MY ONLY CRIME WAS LOYALTY

"The peace process is like a big boat. Everyone wants on it. However there are a few good men who can see the ice berg looming ahead, so they choose to stay on the shore. When the big boat is sinking those on board will remember the men they ridiculed and blackened. They will be the ones still standing on the shore as those who mocked and ridiculed them are drowning, and what good will all the funding in the world be to be them then?"

Jamie Bryson speaking during an interview in 2011 during which he was asked his views on the peace process.

MY ONLY CRIME WAS LOYALTY

"For what shall it profit a man, to gain the whole world but forfeit his own soul?"

Mark 8:36

Printed 2014

Copyright © Jamie Bryson

All rights reserved. No part of this book may be reproduced or transmitted in any form or by any means without written permission from the author, except by a reviewer who wishes to quote brief passages in connection with a review written for insertion in a magazine, newspaper, website or broadcast.

ISBN-13: 978-1502949158

ISBN-10: 1502949156

The author can be followed on Twitter **@JamieBrysonCPNI**

For queries relating to the publishing, distribution or reproduction of any part of this book the Author can be contacted by Email: **JamieBrysonBook@yahoo.co.uk**

CONTENTS

- Acknowledgments **7**
- Forward by Robert Campbell (Ulster Human Rights Watch) **9**
- Introduction **11**

PART ONE:

- Arrested **17**
- Interviewed and Charged **23**
- Bail **39**
- Fighting the conditions **43**
- Case continues **57**
- Welcome to Loyalist North Down **65**
- Ulster Peoples Forum **71**
- The Men Who Don't Exist **85**
- Past, Present and Future **97**

PART TWO:

- The Equality Agenda **105**
- OTR Questions that need to be answered **107**
- End of Freedom **113**
- For God And Ulster **119**
- Traditional Loyalism in Modern Society **123**
- Who Judges the Judges **127**
- Who Judges the Judges Part Two **131**
- Police Ombudsman complaint **135**

Acknowledgements

There are many people that I want to acknowledge and pay tribute to. It is important to have good, loyal people around you in life and it is equally important to return that loyalty.
There are some who cannot be mentioned and there are many things that are unlikely to ever be included in any book.

To my Mother, Father and Grandfather- I thank you for your unconditional love and support. You have been the best family I could ever have wished for.

To my Grandmother who has sadly passed away. I have so many wonderful memories, but most of all I remember the unbelievable human spirit you showed in your final days and hours. I have never seen anything quite so remarkable in my entire life. You showed me the true meaning of faith. The strength of that faith shone brightest in your final hours; you knew that wasn't the end, it was just the beginning. I will see you again someday.
"Safe in the arms of Jesus"

To my Nana- you optimise the meaning of fighting spirit, willpower and battling against the odds. You achieved more in life than I ever will and you are the best and strongest human being that I have ever met. You are my best friend. The unbending spirit inside me that refuses to accept defeat comes from you, I just use mine in a different way. I hope you can be everything to my son that you are to me.

To Esther and my step daughter Abbie- I love you with all my heart, always have and always will.

To my unborn son- I hope that I can be the best Father that you could wish for, just like my Dad was to me. I hope that as you grow older you realise that I wasn't a criminal or a terrorist; I was a patriot who took a stand so as to ensure that your generation would not grow up as second class citizens.

To Jay, Rab, Glen, Roy, Jonto, wee Jim, John Hayes, Josh, Officers & Members of Bangor Protestant Boys Flute Band and associated groups. You never sold your soul for money.
"With our standards flying high, as they were in days gone by".

To the TRUE loyalists in Ulster and our brothers & sisters across the UK - when we all stand together we forever shall be free.

To my true friends, you know who you are.

To Kate Hoey MP for your personal friendship towards me and your loyalty to the Unionist people of our Country.

To Robert (Bertie) Campbell for your friendship and the inspiration you provide. You have dedicated your life to the cause of Ulster- a true hero.

To those who have placed their trust in me and risked their own personal safety to furnish me with documents and information that help to uncover the truth about the false peace, I salute you. I would never betray your confidence.

And finally to all those who cannot be mentioned- your deeds may never fully be disclosed- but know that your commitment and dedication to the cause of Ulster ensures that we remain free to this day.

"And so how far have we now come and how far have we to go?
Those we thought who were our friends- now stand beside the foe
But listen now- the price is high- and they will have to pay
So listen now and heed these words- for we are on our way....."

Foreword

The famous words "Here I stand; I can do no other", attributed to Martin Luther, the champion of the Protestant Reformation when he appeared before the Emperor, Charles V in April 1521 to justify what he had taught and wrote, could be a reflective portrayal of the present attitude, analysis and subsequent actions of Jamie Bryson's experiences as recorded in this book. With refreshing honesty, truthfulness and openness, commodities rarely evident in this province these days, Jamie, without fear or favour 'lays bare', in the most vivid style the corruption which lies with some powers and agencies within Northern Ireland.

Almost two years following the decision by Belfast City Council to limit to eighteen days a year the number of times that the Union Flag (the flag of the United Kingdom) could fly from the City Hall, and the subsequent unionist protests, Jamie, in this book, highlights how he still awaits 'his day in court' to prove his innocence against charges widely suspected by him and the public at large to be 'trumped up' simply in order to neuter the impact of his leadership within his own community.

He also explains in a wider sense, with detailed evidence, how an unprecedented media campaign, aimed at smothering any unionist protests in general and his leadership (real or imagined by the authorities) in particular, which might undermine or unsettle the 'peace process', was devised and implemented by sections of the Press, Police Service of Northern Ireland (PSNI) and the Public Prosecution Service for Northern Ireland (PPS) over the past two years. This evidence demonstrates not only a refusal by the authorities to uphold the right to freedom of peaceful assembly but also portrays the deceptive and disgraceful way they manipulated and distorted facts, and still continue to do so, against any unionist individual or group which rejects the undemocratic system of government which rules, at present, in this part of the United Kingdom.

Unfortunately there is also produced in the book disturbing allegations of collusion between certain unionist parties and individuals who, with the authorities- for their own selfish reasons- continue to assist in the undermining of genuine 'grass root' protest groups such as the Ulster People's Forum (UPF) by promising much but, time after time, proved to have delivered nothing of substance .

In another section of the book Jamie shares with the reader his own very personal feelings and experiences during the past two traumatic years which include continual harassment of him and his immediate family by security sources of dubious backgrounds, a period in jail, numerous court appearances, malicious and concocted smear stories in the media and multiple threats to his life. He also openly and honestly analyses his own strengths and weakness, his successes and failures, his love for his country and his hopes for a Northern Ireland of the future free from violence and at peace with itself.

You are about to read why you should consider your own position in light of these disturbing revelations. Accept the continuing challenge and decide how you can contribute to a realistic future of Unionist security and loyalty in an active and direct manner.

Robert Campbell
Ulster Human Rights Watch

(A friend and proud to be so)

Introduction

People judge me by what they read in the newspapers, by the views of others. Many people despise me and many love me, yet the majority have never met me. They don't know me. That bothers me a bit. People make judgements quickly and stick to them. I suppose in a sense that goes with the territory. You just have to learn to live with it.

There is nothing good about having a public profile, well not the kind that I have anyway. People think it is fun, people think you are egotistical and people think that it must be great to be known. It isn't. I am under constant threat and have to always watch where I go, where I eat and who I socialise with. I wake up every day and leave my house via a reinforced bullet proof steel door- you would need a tank to get in. I walk the short distance to my car and check underneath it. I carry a bullet proof vest which I have to wear regularly. I am warned by the PSNI of threats to my life on a weekly basis. Many of these are intelligence based threats, which means the Police themselves have gained intelligence that I am being targeted. Four people have been charged in the past 12 months alone for threatening to kill me. That is my day. That is reality for me. Does it sound like great fun?

I manage a football team. I can't attend many of their matches because they are played in Catholic areas.

When I go out to socialise I have to bring people with me who are there to keep an eye out for anyone coming to start trouble or to spot security force agents who are trying to covertly gather intelligence or force their way into the company. It is hard to relax. You wouldn't understand until that life becomes your reality. But I knew that would be my life once I put myself out there. I knew there would not be any turning back. I accept that and I accept the consequences that go with it. I always done what I believed was right and if this is the way I have to live my life as a consequence of that then so be it.

A lot of people have a hatred for me that is quite abnormal. They don't know me yet they spend their day sending me hate mail or abusing me on social media. I feel sorry for those people. They must have something lacking in their life that they feel they need to do that.

Some from my own community don't like me either. I don't quite know why. Perhaps it is because the flag protests and some of my campaigning have affected their gravy train. Some are just DUP lackeys and sheep. I don't lose any sleep over it.

When I sat down to write this book it was important I was honest. I have made mistakes at times and throughout the book I have admitted that. If I thought somebody was a clown then I said that. I don't believe in telling lies. I am not a perfect character and nor am I the messiah. I am just an ordinary fella who cares deeply about my Country, my culture and my heritage. There is no shame in that.

I never asked to be at the forefront of the flag protests; I never went looking for that. It just kind of happened. Would I change it? I don't honestly know. There are times I crave the one thing I will now never be able to have in this Country, anonymity. I sometimes wish I could go for a night out or a nice meal in Belfast without looking over my shoulder. I sometimes wish that when I meet people I would just be Jamie to them and they would take me as they find me. But I never hid away in the shadows, I put myself out there publicly so all the consequences of that are on me. No one forced me in front of a camera, no one forced me to take a microphone and address protests. I did that all by myself.

When I say that it just happened let me explain what I mean. I was campaigning for years in the background and I could have ended up doing that for the rest of my life, but the flag protests came along out of nowhere and a political leadership vacuum opened up, I sub consciously moved in to fill it. Or maybe it was consciously, I don't really know. What I do know is all of a sudden I had a platform to articulate and spread the political message I had been preaching without success for so long. I was lucky that way; fate provided me with an opportunity. I took it for better or for worse. I couldn't hand on heart say I would change that mind you, I believe in what I do, I believe in our cause and sometimes standing up for what you believe in has consequences. Do the consequences and affect upon your family outweigh the pull of doing what is right? Evidently they don't or I wouldn't be doing it.

My family have suffered greatly as a result of the stand I have taken; it has put enormous strain on them. I regret that. But I couldn't close my eyes at night knowing what was right and instead of fighting for true peace and freedom for our people, silently go along the road that will lead to the destruction of all I hold dear. That would be cowardly. I would rather live one day as a lion than a thousand as a sheep. I think it used to be painted on the walls of the loyalist wing in the Maze prison *"it's better to die on your feet than live on your knees"*

I have somehow become immune to pressure and stress now, I go for a massage every couple of weeks with Karen, a wonderful woman, and she tells me I sub consciously carry all the stress and tension in my back and shoulders. Some other people have told me I have aged terribly. I don't know about that, but what I do know is that I go to bed every night and sleep like a baby. It doesn't affect me mentally, I don't know whether that is just me or I have built up immunity to it all, but I never find myself lying awake at night or spending my days worrying. I have made peace with myself that what I am doing is right and if I end up suffering or even dead because of that well so be it.

I have a strong faith in God which helps too. I fundamentally believe that not one hair on my head will be harmed unless it is God's will. That gives me an amazing peace inside.

I don't live my life as a Christian should, I am candid about that. I occasionally drink to excess, I have sex outside of marriage and I do things that I am not so sure God would approve of. But you have to make judgements. One day I will face God and give account of my actions. I have made peace with that too.

I am not a diplomat and nor would I want to be. Compromising isn't my style. I don't do it very well. Maybe that is a weakness in my character. When true peace comes to N.Ireland it won't have been made by people like me. I am not a peace maker. If there was true peace in N.Ireland there would be no place for people like me in politics. I aim to expose the sham that is this false peace, and when that battle is won I will ride off into the sunset and let the majority of decent middle of the road Protestants and Catholics come to some kind of arrangement that will see a normal system of Government and a real peace in N.Ireland. A peace that will ensure my children grow up without bitterness in their hearts, but that they will grow up into a society where they can express their culture and identity and others can express theirs without fear of violence or Government oppression. A peace that will see honest politicians- if that is possible- doing what is right for all the people of this Country. There will be no place for terrorists in that land. No place for those who would use their positions to try and destroy the Country from within or wage cultural war on my community.

My heart is full of bitterness and hatred, I have seen what is really going on in this Country and because of that I can never forgive those who have tried to destroy it and nor can I forgive those from my own community who have been complicit in that by their silence. Maybe someday that will change, but that is how I feel at the moment. There is no point lying about it.

You may wonder why I am full of hatred. I missed the IRA's armed terrorism campaign and could be described as a child of peace time. But in that peace time Sinn Fein has done more damage and gained more ground than they ever did prior to that. I have seen that and experienced that. I have taken an active interest and have seen what is really going on, the dirty deals and the secret carve ups that will lead to the destruction of N.Ireland as we know it. I have seen how Sinn Fein and their supporters have been allowed to worm their way into every statutory body and to take control. I am not stupid. I can see what is going on and it isn't good for any self respecting Protestant, Unionist or Loyalist.

I have had elderly ladies who had loved ones blown up, murdered or maimed by the IRA come up to me in tears. They have been betrayed. History is being re-written so the victims are the bad guys and the victim makers are the hero's. That tears my heart out.

Older loyalists sometimes dismiss the viewpoint of my generation as 'ceasefire soldiers'. That is illogical. Do they suggest that because we were born later we somehow don't have an equal stake in our future and our children's future in this Country?

No doubt if I was born 30 years earlier I would have taken up arms to defend Ulster. I have the utmost respect for those who did. They played a major role in ensuring that I didn't grow up on blood stained streets, they used violence to resist violence. What else could they do? They were good people in an impossible situation. They had a choice- let their friends and family die as our Country was blown up and robbed off them- or stand up and fight back. Defending yourself is not terrorism.

In any other Country in the world men and women who took up arms to defend their Country and their people are viewed as patriots.

I am glad that there is no armed conflict and I hope and pray that there never is again. The conflict that my generation will fight will be fought in Courtrooms and political chambers. It will be fought by peaceful protest and resistance. Violence now would be fruitless. It would be a self defeating cycle, it would only end up with my children in the same position that I am in now. I don't want that. The armed fight is over, now it is the fight for peace and that fight cannot be won by restarting the cycle of violence.

By no stretch of the imagination am I a pacifist. If the IRA launched a large scale military campaign tomorrow I would have no hesitation in fighting fire with fire... but it would be fruitless. The IRA knows that. They can never win militarily and therefore we would all end up back at the place we are now, except for the fact that many more coffins would be carried down the streets of Ulster to get there. What is the point in that?

The armed conflict of the generations before me had to be fought. The IRA threw all they had at it and fought to a stalemate. In fact they were on the verge of defeat. They almost overplayed their hand.

That campaign is over and they found out that they cannot win; it leaves us with the battle for the peace, the political battle. It is up to my generation to defeat them in this new battle, and to finish them once and for all.

Perhaps the warped Republican ideal- the cause that inflicted so much violence and destruction upon our Country- will die out with the Provo's.

Maybe this new generation of people from a Roman Catholic and Nationalist background will reject cultural wars and reject the idea that their previous generations fought some kind of just war against the British. Maybe they will simply want to live and let live.

I hope so. Because then I can go and enjoy my life and leave politics to those of my generation who can compromise and build a lasting and prosperous peace. I could leave politics to the politicians and enjoy celebrating my culture from time to time, socialise wherever I wanted, and watch my family grow up in a thriving society where the hatred and bitterness is long gone. Maybe then I could put all my hatred and the desire to resist the system in a glass cage with the words 'break in the event of war' on it.

I bear no shame, I resisted.

Jamie Bryson
October 2014

Arrested

"I found him, I found him, I found him" screamed the overly excited, ginger haired Police officer who entered the unlocked bedroom in Pastor Mark Gordon's house on 28th February 2013. I couldn't help but laugh at this officer as he jumped up and down like a little schoolgirl- ready to execute an arrest that you could see meant a lot to him.

He forcefully pulled me up from the bed where I was casually relaxing and called to a female Officer that I was now in his possession. She seemed slightly embarrassed by the antics of the uniformed sergeant who was continuing to behave as if he had just found Bin Laden. She cautioned me under Section 46 of the Serious Crime Act for 'Encouraging or assisting offenders' and also under the Public Processions Act. While these pieces of legislation meant little to me at the time, they were to become the centre piece in one of the most bizarre and politically motivated criminal cases ever to enter an N.Ireland courtroom.

I was handcuffed and pulled down the stairs. On the second staircase I passed my friend Pastor Mark Gordon; I said loudly that this episode would not have looked out of place in Nazi Germany. These comments were later to be attributed to Mark in a bizarre court case in which the PSNI and PPS sought to prosecute him for 'obstruction'. They lost and the case caused maximum humiliation to the PSNI, but more of that later.

As I was lead out of Marks home, I recognised four uniformed Police Officers in the garden. They were good guys, former RUC men who looked ashamed to be playing any part in this quite obviously politically motivated and contrived arrest. I nodded to them and smiled. I held no anger or grudge towards them: they were only doing their job.

However, their sergeant was a different animal. He had a clear personal vendetta and clearly seemed to enjoy the perceived power he felt his job gave him.

I was then put into a Police car to make the journey to Musgrave PSNI station. A few locals came out and shouted 'No Surrender' as the car began to move off.

The two detectives who transported me to Musgrave were attached to the now discredited DULCET team which- in my mind- was set up to persecute the Protestant flag protestors and was headed up by Sean Wright. I don't have much time for Sean Wright. He formerly led some high profile murder investigations- now he is pursuing Protestants for what amounts to little more than jay walking. That tells me all I need to know about Sean Wright.

The officers accompanying me were fine and did not seem to have any personal agenda or political agenda. It was obvious from their body language that they felt the whole thing was little more than a political move designed to take some of the sting out of the flag protests. Obviously I concurred.

Finally I arrived at Musgrave Street PSNI station. It had taken the PSNI 48 hours, 2 helicopters, 18 Police Cars not to mention countless officers but finally they had their man. They had arrested me under legislation designed to deal with Islamist hate preachers who encouraged terrorism. They adapted it to encouraging an unnotified public procession, even though they themselves were still seeking judicial clarity over whether the weekly processions were actually illegal or not.

On the evening prior to the original PSNI raid on my home on the 27th February, senior PSNI officers held a meeting with a Sinn Fein delegation, which included convicted terrorists such as Old Bailey bomber Gerry Kelly. He demanded 'action', Sinn Fein called the tune and the PSNI played it. The PSNI tried to deny that other IRA leaders attended the meeting but their names had to be released when the court ordered disclosure. This incident is covered in full in a later chapter of the book, perhaps the one chapter that the PSNI would love to ensure never seen the light of day! So here I was, arrested and about to be processed. Bravo PSNI, Bravo!

From the morning of the 27th to tea time on the 28th February I had some fun. I laughed, as did many others, at the PSNI's expense. Some people said I should just hand myself in, the Co. Down Spectator said I responded *"would you have asked the Jews to hand themselves into the Nazis".*

I was at home in the bathroom of my house in Donaghadee when I saw the PSNI land rovers driving up the street leading to my home.
I had a fair idea they would be coming: after all Gerry Kelly had demanded action.

I picked up some essentials and headed out the backdoor to a nearby house. From here I watched the PSNI gain entry to my house and begin their search. They had summoned my mother home to open the door.

I rang my mother's phone and asked to speak to the officer in charge; I asked him if there was a warrant for my arrest? He said he just wanted to speak to me. I asked again was there a warrant? The officer said there was not a warrant for my arrest. Armed with the knowledge that the PSNI had told me there was no warrant for my arrest there was no way I was ever going to voluntarily hand myself over to them. Why should I? The whole thing was a complete sham and I was going to exploit it for all it was worth.

Half an hour later the news broke on the BBC. The PSNI had made a statement saying they had arrested me. They hadn't. The pantomime takes another twist.

I was in the habit of varying where my car was parked due to threats from Republicans. So I casually got into my car- out of sight of the PSNI- and drove to Kilcooley where I met up with Pastor Gordon. I took a series of calls from various media outlets who were understandably confused as to how I was able to answer my phone. After all hadn't the PSNI issued a statement claiming I had been arrested!

The media soon picked up on the embarrassment of the situation for the PSNI and began asking questions. The Police subsequently backtracked and said there was no arrest warrant but there was a search warrant that would have allowed them to arrest me if I was at home when they entered, which I wasn't.

It all seemed like a massive cock up on the PSNI's part.

I left my car in Kilcooley and travelled with Pastor Gordon to Newtownards where we stopped for a fry in a local Cafe. I was approached by some locals who recognised me and had heard the news. They offered their full support and voiced their disdain for the PSNI.

During my fry I took a call from Barrie Halliday, Willie Frazer's pastor. Barrie advised me that William had been arrested at his home that morning and the raid was continuing in Markethill. Instinctively I knew that this was quickly becoming a political witch hunt.

After breakfast we travelled back to Kilcooley. After only a few minutes some locals came in to advise that 'Kelly's heroes' had swamped the estate on a massive scale. They surrounded the community offices and seized my car. They had no warrant or lawful right to seize the car but in their obvious desperation they ploughed on ahead anyway. Detectives swarmed into the car park at Kilcooley shops desperate to rectify their earlier mistake and put to bed an arrest operation that was quickly becoming a damage limitation exercise.

Some people said that I escaped in the boot of a car driven by a female friend.

The PSNI searched the offices and surrounding area bemused as to why they could not find me. One officer became irritated and shouted *"He's not f**king Houdini, find him"*. The pressure was beginning to tell on some officers, and it was only 11am on the 27th February.

At 11:30am I filmed the now infamous video that the PSNI quoted time and time again during bail hearings. I taunted the PSNI, I wound them up and I readily admit that. What they were doing to me- and had done to hundreds of other peaceful protestors- was sickening and despicable. They were acting under pressure from known members of the IRA and there was no way I was willingly going to play along with their contrived operation.

They found the video very embarrassing and I'm proud of that. They deserved it. They deserved to be utterly humiliated and exposed for what they were doing. Only a fool would play along in silence. The video wasn't one of my most articulate bits of speaking, in fact it came across as a rant; but I was furious and disgusted that this so called British police force would behave in such an oppressive manner.

The video instantly went viral on social media and many supportive loyalists began taunting the PSNI, I was jokingly given the title of 'hide and seek champion'. PSNI officers began contacting local community workers begging for information as to my whereabouts. They were told where to go, and rightly so.

Around 2pm some people suggested that the PSNI called at a property in which I was sitting having lunch. It was said that I escaped through a rear exit, over a hedge and into another nearby house.

Sharon O'Neil from UTV got in touch wanting an interview. I didn't mind Sharon, I didn't think she would stitch me up, and nor she did. She came to a house in which I had earlier had my lunch, which some people say had been disturbed by the presence of the PSNI. I was travelling around in the boot of cars at this stage. I had left the property for a quick meeting and returned to meet Sharon.

We done the interview and I answered her questions. I didn't look great and if truth be told I didn't feel great either. I was tired, I needed a rest.

I ended up at a house in Kilcooley around 8pm, some locals might not have noticed me going in, it has been alleged that I was dressed as a woman. That particular house had already been raided twice on that day, I figured they wouldn't come back a third time.

Not long after I arrived the police again swamped the area. Neighbours said they saw a woman who looked a lot more like a man walking by a stationary police patrol.

It has been alleged I was in the attic of a house right under the PSNI's noises then the PSNI got a call to tell them I had been seen elsewhere and they sped off as quickly as could.

The third raid in 7 hours yielded nothing for the PSNI. I went to bed and watched a DVD. I received some text messages showing pictures of graffiti that had went up across North down, it read- 'PSNI disgrace, couldn't catch baby face'. I went to sleep, safe in the knowledge that whatever happened the following day, the PSNI had suffered a major embarrassment.

They launched a manhunt that would be more apt for a serial killer. The longer it went on the more resources they wasted. It all adds up. They brought it on themselves. Had the PSNI contacted my solicitor and asked me to come in for a Voluntary interview all this would have been avoided. They chose the IRA pleasing stunt. It backfired, spectacularly.

28 February started early. I had arranged meetings with members of the Ulster Peoples Forum. I gave my view that all contact with the PSNI should be broken. They agreed and a statement was issued to that effect.

The Ulster Peoples Forum was a legitimate and lawful political pressure group. The PSNI treated it as if it was a major terrorist organisation. But that is all to come.

That afternoon, the local PSNI Commander Nigel Grimshaw got in contact. He had initially contacted Tatty and asked him to get in touch with me. I told Tatty he could give him one of the numbers I was using- I changed sim cards every 4 or 5 hours during those couple of days.

Nigel said he wanted to *"end the circus."* He promised a favourable attitude to bail if I handed myself in. I couldn't do that. It would be like making a deal with the devil.

I knew the PSNI would find me and anyhow, they could not be anymore embarrassed than they already had been.

I spoke to Stephen Nolan and done an extensive interview with him. It has never been published.

Not long after this I went up to the main bedroom in Marks house. I lay on the bed and made a few telephone calls. Then there was a thunderous knock on the door.

After that came the much disputed PSNI version of events as to how they came to enter the house. Their statements were all conflicting in Court during Marks contest hearing. I think some of them lied. It's not illegal to think. Some people demand that you don't say it is lies they tell, but why shouldn't one have the right to honestly say what he or she thinks- I think many PSNI officers lie quite often.

Look at recent history in Omagh where PSNI officers were torn apart in Court for lying. That is not isolated, believe me. It is widespread and it is rampant. There is a culture of bending the truth that runs through a section of the PSNI.

There were a few statements missing from the arrest operation. There were no statements made by the officers in the garden. They were principled and decent old school RUC lads. Maybe they just weren't asked to make a statement, some people said to me that they refused to. One thing is for sure, they wouldn't have lied.

There are many decent men and women in the PSNI who were formerly of an RUC background but missed Patton so had to stay in. They despise what the once proud RUC has become; I know this because many of them regularly tell me.

Then there are other officers- most of whom joined the PSNI following Patten- and they bring nothing but shame and disgrace upon those who went before them.

Good RUC officers lost their lives fighting the IRA and now we have a police force that more often than not is working to the agenda of those who murdered and maimed the security forces for decades. Where did it all go wrong?

Mark won his Court case. He was denied legal aid. He had to pay out of his own pocket to challenge the PSNI lies.

They offered him a caution if he just pleaded guilty. No court and no costs. It was the easy embarrassment free way for all concerned. He said no, fought them and won. That is the man of principle I am proud to call my friend.

Interviewed & Charged

I arrived at Musgrave Street to be processed. The car journey had been eventful. The two officers were okay- they smiled in agreement when I joked about the conduct of the local sergeant- I think they knew he was a clown.

I knew the concocted PSNI charges would be made to stick for the time being one way or another. I was not to know just how comical the entire process was about to become.

I want to clear up one point: I refused food in Police custody because I do not trust the PSNI. I did not go on hunger strike and then order an Indian curry. I don't even eat Indian food. That entire story was a figment of the imagination of some newspaper 'source'. It was a lot of nonsense.

I was pleased to see my solicitor arrive, Darren Duncan. He is in my mind the best available in his profession. I wouldn't change him for anyone. I told the Police when I arrived: I want Darren and only Darren or I wouldn't be engaging in any interviews. He has represented me for many years. I regard him as more than just a solicitor; I would call him a friend.

The interviews, which you can hear in full audio online, began around nine o'clock. They were comical. The Police clearly did not understand the Public Processions Act and the two officers sent to conduct the interviews were ill prepared or wildly out of their depth. I was amazed- as was Darren- at what they were putting forward.

To be fair, the officers seemed like decent guys and they looked slightly embarrassed by the situation. I am not sure they really wanted to be there.

Here I was after a massive police manhunt- charged under Serious Crime legislation- and the PSNI were throwing down screenshots of the Ulster Peoples Forum website and demanding to know if I was a member of the group.

They then moved on to the 'serious crime' that I had encouraged. They said that when I spoke at City Hall and said the *"the Protestant people must all move forward together"* that what I really meant was that they should form up and have an illegal procession. Yes I know how it sounds, but that was the base of the charge, the evidence of serious crime.

I couldn't believe how farcical the whole interview process was. The PSNI were smart in how they abused and twisted a piece of legislation designed for serious crime and adapted it to what could at best be described as a minor offence akin to jay walking.

Later I will highlight the folly of this particular approach, because the PPS and PSNI backed themselves into an embarrassing corner whilst fighting tooth and nail to ensure that I remained on silencing bail conditions. They didn't want me able to speak out and detail the reality of these 'charges'. They knew how laughable they were and they knew from word go that the serious crime charges would never see the inside of a courtroom. They needed a way of silencing me and contriving a charge around the Serious Crime Act in theory give them a way to throw in outrageous bail conditions that would have shamed Joseph Stalin. This is how the PSNI do business.

The interviews continued into the following day. By this stage I heard that Willie had been refused bail. But even more shocking was that IRA terrorist Sean Hughes had received bail without any PSNI objections. I was amazed. Two men from South Armagh- one a victim and one a victim maker- and the PSNI strenuously object to bail in the case of the victim and happily agree to bail for the victim maker.

The interviews continued in the same laughable fashion. They focused on the public processions. I quizzed them on what the legislation was and they told me three different versions during three interviews. Truth is they didn't know.

I am not being boastful when I say I tied them in knots. They were like lambs to the slaughter, sent down to try and contrive a charge for a so called offence that the PSNI had facilitated.

I informed them of the meetings between the Ulster Peoples Forum and senior command of the PSNI, and how at those meetings the PSNI had actually encouraged the so called processions to take a particular direction. They couldn't find the minutes, or so they said. Then they said there were no minutes. The PPS stuck to this line for seventeen months before all of sudden minutes appeared ... minutes that previously didn't exist.

Around 9pm I was officially charged. You are meant to get a fair impartial hearing in front of the custody sergeant in regards to police bail. The interviewing officer spent half an hour briefing the custody sergeant before I was brought up. It was like asking Al Capone to investigate the Mafia. I knew the score, there would be no police bail and nor did I want it.

It is interesting that before I was charged the BBC had already received a statement from the PSNI saying that I had been charged and would appear in Court in the morning. That shows you just how transparent the so called 'police bail' hearing was.

A long term mistruth that has been perpetuated by some opponents of my political viewpoint is that I told everyone to refuse bail. That is an absolute fabrication, I never said that. That was a sensationalist headline and if you go back and read the interview in the Irish News you will see that is not what I said.

What I say was that the PSNI were abusing the bail system in the police station by slapping outrageously oppressive conditions on people that a Court would never have permitted. I said that people should refuse bail from the police station and instead ask to be brought before Judge the following day. This way any conditions imposed would be subject to judicial scrutiny. The **"don't take bail go to jail"** headline was a gross misrepresentation of what I said. I suppose many of my critics know this but it suits their agenda to peddle the lie that I told everyone to refuse bail and then applied for bail myself. The facts tell the truth: I suggest some people take the time to go back and read what I actually said.

I told my solicitor I wouldn't be taking police bail. He said that was fine but we should hear their objections anyway. I went up to listen and ended up laughing. One of the objections was that I could *"interfere with suspects"*. It was almost a battle between me and my solicitor to see who could inform the PSNI officer that no such objection was valid or even logical. I managed to tell him first. The look on the officer's face was hilarious as was that on the face of the female custody sergeant. It was a circus and we had just indentified our first two clowns. Bail was refused. The other objections were hilarious; they portrayed me as a dangerous terrorist, a threat to National Security. I smiled a reluctant smiled. It pleased me to know that the people's protests were having such an affect.

The civilian guards in the station were amazingly supportive and I found their backing greatly encouraging. One woman opened my cell door around mid-night and she said *"I just wanted to see you and to tell you that we are all behind you. It's a disgrace what they are doing to you and Willie."* I appreciated that. It's something I will never forget, a small gesture that will stay with me and I won't forget.

I had got a pen and some paper from the custody desk to write some letters. I hadn't eaten in almost 72 hours and wasn't feeling good at all; the tone of the letters probably reflected that. The words I wrote came from the heart.

I dozed off into a sleep, strangely contented. I had seen all their evidence and I knew it was a joke. It was political and it was contrived. I knew the PSNI would never want it seeing the inside of the Courtroom.

Almost two years later an amazing piece of information came to light. On the day I was charged Karen Quinlivin QC addressed Belfast High Court in relation to the weekly walks. She said *"Matters have deteriorated in the sense that there is quite clearly an impasse in which [police] call for judicial clarity in relation to this issue."*

I was already in Custody and charged yet Mr Justice Treacy in the High Court agreed with the QC's assessment for the need for judicial clarity. I was in custody and charged while the Judiciary was still seeking to provide clarity on whether the weekly walks I was charged with had been illegal or not. It shines a light on the clear abuse of lawful process, when the High Court was hearing a case so as to try and give clarity on whether the weekly walks were legal or not, the PSNI charged me anyway and objected venomously to bail.

When I woke up the next morning I was invited to take a shower and have a shave. The razor was a bit rough so I declined the shave but gratefully took a long shower.

Jim Dowson had been charged the previous evening. When I was brought out into the van in handcuffs- like some kind of dangerous terrorist- I caught site of Jim already locked up. I had to laugh. The PSNI hadn't even tried to hide the political nature of their actions. They quite brazenly just happened to scoop three of the most high profile protestors inside 48 hours.

Mind you, they didn't quite understand the protests: they didn't belong to me or to anyone else. I had no greater status than anyone else standing on the street protesting. Everyone was equal. The protests belonged to the people but what the PSNI sought to do was to remove those who communicated on behalf of the protestors so as to be able to replace people like me with spokespeople who would be a lot more amenable to protecting the process.

The people that played their part in that contrived little move should hang their heads in shame. Those who claimed to be our friends yet conspired with the Government to have us removed know who they are. They carry the shame for their actions; I do not need to say anymore than that.

I was brought up into the Court for my first bail hearing, the continuation of the circus. A Police officer took to the stand and began with a lie. He said I was found in a locked attic. The Judge quoted this when she summed up her reasoning for refusing bail. He then went on to say if released I might appear on the Nolan show. Yes really. Then he said I had too great an influence to be allowed out into a delicate situation.

It is strange that only four days previously Mark McEwan- the PSNI area commander- had telephoned me and asked me to use my positive influence to ensure everything passed of peacefully at the protest held outside PSNI headquarters. Two weeks before that, the PSNI had released a statement into the media praising the positive influence of the Ulster Peoples Forum in trying to keep protests legal. They seemed to develop convenient amnesia. Well that is the polite way to put it. What I really thought is that they were a bunch of lying bastards who were politically compromised. Nothing has happened since to convince me otherwise.

The Judge was a coward in my opinion; she was scared to stand up to the PSNI, even though it was obvious that the whole thing was a politically contrived farce. She played along with it. The Judiciary is supposed to protect the private citizen from abuses of lawful process; instead I feel the Judge became part of the political cabal. She failed me in her duty to act as the final bulwark between freedom and tyranny. That is my honest personal opinion. I am sure the Judge wont like that, but why should I lie? The book is telling the true story about how I felt and what happened. I am not going to sugar coat it.

I was remanded into custody and put in the prison van to travel to HMP Maghaberry. I wasn't thrilled to be going to jail. Anyone who says they enjoy going to jail or that it is a breeze is lying. It's horrible. Looking out the window of the prison van I asked myself one simple question: If I had the power to go back and change things would I do it all again? The answer was a resounding yes. I had done what I'd done and taken the stand I took because I believed it was right. If I had to go to jail as a consequence of that then so be it.

I was put into a single cell. There was no shortage of Catholic hoods on the Bann House committal wing. They seemed to put their day in shouting abuse at me through the windows of their cell. They informed me I was a dead man, that they would murder me in the yard and that I was nobody. The irony that they passed their day shouting at me telling me I was nobody was not lost on me: I was that much of a nobody that they shouted about me all day. I just sat back in my cell and laughed. Some of it was quite funny. Willie Frazer was across the other side of the wing. He spent his day shouting back at them. I must say it provided entertainment.

My first night remanded was a Saturday. I watched the news and saw that my mum had addressed the rally at City Hall. I was so proud. My mother is a moderate woman, in no way political or sectarian, but she knew the difference between right and wrong.

After a number of days Willie and I were transferred into double cell. It was the first time I had got a face to face chat with him since our arrests. Willie thought that the cell could be bugged so we refrained from talking about too much.

It was no secret that there had been some tension between us over the direction of the protests and I talk about that particular period elsewhere in this book. However, I had always liked Willie Frazer. I had worked alongside him for a couple of years prior to the protest. I often joke and call this period the wilderness years, a time when nobody wanted to hear voices such as ours. The peace train- and the gravy train that ran parallel to it- were just too good to be true. People ignored our warnings, dismissed us as idiots. I am sure many now wished they had listened.

We had a long discussion walking around the yard about the evidence the PSNI had put before us. His case appeared just as comical as mine. They did find a taser gun in his house. This led the other prisoners to christen him 'Tazer Frazer'. I found that one quite amusing. Willie could take a joke and enjoyed a bit of banter, very little fazed him. Soon I was myself calling him "Tazer". The name stuck.

We spent a lot of time piecing together the timeline leading up to our arrest and found much that disturbed us. I still feel today there were hidden hands at play throughout the whole protest. Government agents were trying to put things back on track, when they failed they resorted to mass arrests. It was legalised internment.

The Governments intelligence analysts didn't see the protests coming. They thought they had loyalism boxed in and bought off. They didn't realise that those who were taking the thirty pieces of silver didn't speak for everyone. In fact they spoke for only a minority. When those champions of the process sat around the table with statutory bodies they told the Government how things were all rosy in the garden. The Government believed them. Then came the flag protests and a new generation of loyalism sprung up. No one ever expected that.

My first visit in the prison was one of my closest friends, Tatty Gordon. To many others he is Pastor Mark Gordon. To me he is Tatty. He brought along with him Esther, who is due to give birth to our child in February 2015. We had been in a long term relationship and then fell out for a couple of years. Prior to my arrest we had been back in touch. There was much I had to discuss with Tatty so we got all that out of the way and then Tatty left me alone with Esther for the final ten minutes. He is good that way, always thinking about the needs of others and never wanting to intrude. His ability to place himself in someone else's shoes is one of his qualities that I really appreciate. Tatty did every single thing I asked him to do for me whilst I was in prison. Some days I bombarded him with requests to do things for me, he never once said no. Every time he visited he left a generous amount of money in for me. He didn't have to do that.

It was Tatty that brought me into politics when I left school, for four years he trained me at Kilcooley Forum where I worked as his assistant. When I was in prison Tatty sent me a letter. In that later he said he was proud of me and proud to call me his friend. That meant a lot to me.

You only ever get a handful of real friends in life, and Tatty Gordon is certainly one of those people.

I have lots of mates, very few friends. And that's the way I like it.

My family had held a meeting with Peter Robinson just a few days after my arrest. They came to visit me not long after Tatty and Esther came for the committal visit. My family worked tirelessly to campaign for me. I could never repay them for that.

At the time I said that Peter Robinson would use my arrest to make a grandstand and portray himself as standing up for the loyalist people. I knew exactly what he was doing. Perhaps my family just weren't as cynical as I was and they believed that the First Minister of the Country genuinely cared about my welfare. I still wrote to Peter when I got out thanking him for coming out publicly in support of me. I gave him the benefit of the doubt but in my heart I continue to believe that he was only playing a political game and using me as a pawn.

Local MLA Alex Easton tried to help. He is a decent man, though I think he would get far further forward if he didn't try and please everyone. I have had many arguments with Alex, including one which ended with us squaring up to each other during the local Council election in May 2014. I had been gloating on social media about the electoral hit taken by the DUP. Alex made a jibe over lunchtime saying *"sure you came running to the DUP to get you out of jail"*. I completely flipped. I have never run to anyone in my life, let alone the DUP. Alex had made this jibe in front of some DUP wannabes that hang of his every word. I view them as clowns. These are the type of people who sit on social media giving it loads, yet if you approach them with a challenge, they lock themselves in their house for four days. These are the kind of people who speak of Peter Robinson as some kind of God as if thou shall not criticise the anointed one. These people to me are blind followers. I waited until Alex was in the corridor and then I confronted him. The row got heated and words were exchanged. A whole raft of issues exploded that went as deep as the DUP's agreement to John Larkin being appointed as Attorney General. Larkin then appointed Barra McGrory, an appointment I continue to strongly oppose. I shouldn't have taken all those frustrations out on Alex, it wasn't his fault. He is a great constituency worker and really does try and help people with their day to day issues, but I felt he overstepped the mark with his jibe. It was untrue regardless of anything else.

In hindsight Alex was probably frustrated at how the election was playing out for the DUP and made a jibe to rile me, things then got heated and words were exchanged. I haven't spoken to Alex much since that incident, which is a shame because I genuinely do like him. We did briefly engage over the Twelfth of July for discussions about the protest to be held in Bangor after the parade. That didn't end well either. One of his hangers on, who happens to be a local Deputy Master of the Orange Order went into a flap because our band stood for more than three minutes. The three minutes was a joke anyway, I thought it was pathetic.

I thought the whole graduated response was pathetic. I believed at the time it was nothing more than mainstream Unionism trying to take control of the situation and get us over the Twelfth. I kept my mouth shut. I thought to myself *'say nothing Jamie or you will be the worst in the world. If people want to believe their crap then let them, it's not your problem.'* I should have spoken up at the time. I regret not challenging it. They sold the people a pup. It was graduated surrender.

Sometimes I tell myself to keep my mouth shut. Just let them get on with it. Maybe I should, perhaps that would serve me better. I just cannot seem to accept the crap that is spewed to the Protestant people, I can see exactly what is going on so why should I silently just go along with it? If I just silently go along with it then in my mind I become no better than the DUP sheep I so detest, people who can't think for themselves.

The Orange Deputy Master continued flapping and then waved the Orangemen and bandsmen behind us and told them to just march around us. I couldn't believe it. I was fuming. This coward, after men fought and died for our freedom this clown is waving for fellow Protestants to march around their own people, lest they upset the PSNI. Fair play to those behind us, they told him to sling his hook.

That was the last real engagement I had with Alex. I am led to believe that elements of the Robinson camp in the DUP blamed him for leaking me confidential DUP information about their party meetings. That was the information from the supposedly secret meeting that prompted the sacking of Edwin Poots. I can assure those inside the Robinson camp that Alex Easton has never provided me any information. He is fiercely loyal to Peter and those in that wing of the DUP. That in fact is one of the reasons Alex and I politically do not see eye to eye.

When Peter Robinson made some public comments supporting me he drew stinging criticism from all the non Unionist political parties. They said it was interfering with the judicial process. I had to laugh, just what was Spike Murray doing when he met the Chief Constable the night before my arrest? Or what was Gerry Adams doing ringing Downing Street to demand the release of an IRA terrorist? I am under no illusion; the Provo's pushed at an open door when they told the Chief Constable to take certain courses of action.

I had a High Court bail hearing on the Friday, just a few days after Peter Robinson publicly expressed the feeling that there was a great disparity in how the PSNI, the PPS and the Judiciary dealt with Loyalists and Republicans. I found this ironic given that it was Peter Robinson and the DUP that paved the way for the former solicitor of half the IRA Army Council and all the IRA OTR's to become DPP. In my opinion it was the sordid betrayal at Hillsborough that allowed justice to be surrendered into the hands of IRA placemen.

Nevertheless Peter came out and criticised the current bias being shown. It's no more than he should have done because it was absolutely blatant. Nigel Dodd's raised my case and that of Willie Frazer in Parliament with the Secretary Of State. A nice gesture, but the Secretary of State doesn't have clean hands in how the PSNI dealt with the likes of me. The Secretary of State has been no friend of Unionism. I do not forget that it was she who first said that the flag protests had become a National Security situation which effectively gave the PSNI cart Blanche to wade into peaceful protestors with batons and rubber bullets.

As I arrived at the video link for my High Court bail hearing I met Richard McConkey for the first time. He was to be my Barrister. Being our first encounter I wasn't sure what to make of him. That was then. Now, I would never allow another Barrister to represent me. Over the course of my case he has been nothing short of outstanding. Never afraid to challenge the continuous lies perpetuated by the PSNI and PPS. He has devoted much of his personal time to fighting this politically contrived case. I have the utmost respect for Richard McConkey. Both him and my solicitor Darren Duncan care about justice. They aren't just there to make money, they care about people and they know the difference between right and wrong. That is probably why they will never end up working for the PPS- I would think they would struggle to peddle the lies that often come from PPS representatives.

The PPS Barrister took the stand for my High Court bail hearing and quoted from the online video I posted when the PSNI were looking for me. She said I called the PSNI Fascists and Nazis. Yes I did say that, and I am glad I did because that is the way they behaved. She demeaned the character reference given by Tatty in his capacity as a Pastor and she referred to how he obstructed police. She was a disgrace. Tatty Gordon was found not guilty in his subsequent court appearance. I remembered how her face looked so spiteful when she was after embarrassed at the point I won a wonderful face victory over the PPS and PSNI in my bail variation High Court hearing (which paved the way for everyone's bail conditions to be lifted for the Twelfth of July parades, and pleased me no end). She wasn't just doing her job: she seemed full of hatred. I enjoyed seeing her squirm on the day Justice Weir ripped them apart. She deserved that. On the occasion of my bail application it was her that came out on top mind you. The Judge was a disgrace in my view. Having formerly represented the Parades Commission, he was presiding over a case dealing with someone who was charged in relation to parading issues. He then went off on a rant about how the Judiciary should not be political spending seven minutes on this political rant. Sammy Wilson called him an arrogant civil servant or words to that affect, I fully agreed. The Judge has been given a role in the judicial system and he is meant to protect people like me from political persecution. Instead he joined in and used a hearing to deal with the serious matter of my liberty to grandstand and give his political view. He refused me bail, but then again he was always refusing me bail. That is what I believe. It got Peter Robinson plenty of publicity.

I went back across to my cell and knew then that it would be a prolonged staff. Requesting to see the Governor, I asked to be transferred to the dedicated wing for loyalist prisoners. I was moved within hours.

The loyalist wing was a lot easier. I knew quite a few of the lads already and met some new faces. I found them all good lads.

I spent much of my time talking to Michael Stone. I decided to make my own mind up on 'Stoner'. I quickly came to the conclusion that Michael Stone is not mad, he is not insane. He is an extremely intelligent man with a much clearer grasp on what is really going on in this Country than many of those who seek to dismiss him. One thing that will live with me forever is when I asked him if he regretted the stand he took for Ulster because it had ended up with him spending much of his adult life in prison. Michael simply said "I did what I had to do. I had my best thirty years on the outside". If Michael Stone was a republican there would be massive campaigns to have him released, sadly many within Unionism seem to have forgotten about him and others are probably happy to let him rot in prison. I hope that one day Michael Stone can once again be a free man.

Whilst on the wings I wrote to a few different people. There was a person corresponded every day. I will never forget that. I wrote a few poems, I think the person I sent them to still have them. My family visited me all the time even through it wasn't easy for them. It isn't easy for any family.

Compared to others I did very little time in prison. Men have done 20 years or more for what they believe in. Those are men who have sacrificed for their Country. They have my utmost respect. I didn't deserve to be in prison. I was interned via remand and the fact I was high profile probably brought it to the point where the PSNI and PPS could no longer justify keeping me in prison. There are many other protestors whose cases weren't constantly in the media and being highlighted. Their human rights were abused as well. It should never be forgotten that many peaceful protestors have been treated just as badly as me but haven't been in a position to expose the wrongdoing perpetrated against them. Those people have paid a price for defending the flag of their Country too.

I am no hero: this is not what this book is about. The book is about highlighting one case and showing people what the State do to political dissenters and those who are viewed as destabilising the political process. If they do it to me then they will do it to anyone. It may be Jamie Bryson the hard line loyalist today but tomorrow it could be the investigative journalist or any other individual who the Government see as a threat.

I only did the same as thousands of others. My crime was the same as theirs: loyalty.

Timeline of my arrest

- On 31st Jan PSNI issued a statement after meeting a UPF delegation, of which I was part. PSNI said they welcomed that *"Lawful, peaceful protest was being encouraged and agreed to meet the UPF leaders in the future"* At no stage do the PSNI say that the weekly walks had been illegal. In fact during this meeting they had said quite the opposite. It seems quite bizarre that PSNI would issue this statement on 31st Jan 2013 praising the UPF for positive leadership and welcoming the fact we sought to ensure all protests remained lawful, and then arrest the Chairman of the UPF and object to bail because of *"Encouraging or assisting offenders"*. This change in tactic came of course following IRA terrorists Gerry Kelly, Sean Murray and Martin McGuinness demanding that the leadership of the protest movement was removed.

- On 1st Feb 2013 Mr Justice Treacy had granted leave for a Judicial Review in relation to whether the weekly walks from East Belfast to City Hall had been illegally facilitated by PSNI or not. Justice Treacy also said that he was unsure about whether Court proceedings were appropriate. This shows that there was not even judicial clarity on 1st Feb 2013. It seems to be a fundamental abuse of British Justice to bring charges against a person when neither the PSNI nor the Judiciary could provide clarity at the time of the alleged offences about whether the alleged act was unlawful or not.

- In policing board minutes of 7th Feb it was raised about police inconsistency in facilitation of community reps negotiating with protestors. I was part of a delegation to meet the policing board and raise these concerns. I informed policing board members at their HQ that I felt their needed to be safeguards for those of us PSNI were asking to intervene. None was forthcoming from PSNI. Entrapment?

- In policing board minutes of 7 Feb the Chief Constable confirmed he had written to the Parades Commission seeking guidance. Senior police also directly say in the minutes that *"The legal definition of processions is not clear"*. PSNI senior management tell the Policing Board on 7th Feb that the legal definition was not clear, so how could the ordinary citizen, especially one who was been encouraged to use his perceived influence to keep the weekly walks peaceful, be expected to know?

- On morning of 26 Feb 2013 Peter Osborne of the Parades Commission tells the PSNI the Parades Commission had no role to play in the weekly walks. It was following this that PSNI began to go back and arrest people for walks which they had facilitated, in the context of the PSNI being unaware of the law. Why then hasn't PSNI offices facilitating these walks been charged?

- SF/IRA met the Chief Constable and demanded "action" on the night of 26 Feb 2013. The following morning (27 Feb) the PSNI sought (and failed until 28) to arrest William Frazer and myself.

- In an online blog published by Convicted IRA terrorist and MLA Gerry Kelly on 27 Feb 2013 (co-incidentally the day of my attempted arrest which was the morning after he claimed to have told Chief Constable to take action) he said that PSNI had told the policing board that *"there is no such thing as an illegal parade"*. G Kelly also said that the Chief Constable refused to describe the weekly walks as "illegal". Again this shows that the PSNI had been sending out confusing messages.

- Gerry Kelly said in his blog that SF/IRA wanted figures of how many arrests there had been in relation to what he termed 'illegal marches'. He said this request was to be answered at next policing board meeting. It was after this request from SF/IRA that the PSNI decided to arrest hundreds of people for marches they had previously facilitated.

- On 1st March (the day before my bail hearing) Karen Quinlivin QC- solicitor acting for Republicans from Short Strand in the Judicial review case- was quoted in the Newsletter following the previous day's High Court hearing. She had told the Court *"Matters have deteriorated in the sense that there is quite clearly an impasse in which [police] call for judicial clarity in relation to this issue"*. I was already in Custody and charged yet Mr Justice Treacy in the High Court agreed with Ms Quinlivin's assessment on the need for judicial clarity. I was in custody and charged on 1 March while the

Judiciary was still seeking to provide judicial clarity on whether the weekly walks I was charged with had been illegal or not. It shines a light on the clear abuse of lawful process: The High Court was bringing forward a case so as to try and give clarity on whether the weekly walks were legal or not but the PSNI charged me anyway and objected venomously to bail. The Magistrate then agreed with the ludicrous PSNI objections and refused bail on 2 March. I was effectively jailed on the basis that the PSNI did not know whether I had broken the law or not, so they decided to just pre-empt the High Court and give their own judicial clarity. At this stage the PSNI not only sought to control the political arena but they had also taken to providing their own politically expedient interpretations of the law.

Bail

I finally got bail. The PSNI changed their objections to bail after relentless political pressure. Much of this pressure came from Jim Allister, Tom Elliott and members of the PUP. Robert Campbell- who has written the forward for this book- worked tirelessly behind the scenes as did Michael Copeland MLA.

I was told that Sean Wright, the detective in charge of the DULCET team had agreed bail conditions with my solicitor, Darren, who told me these conditions were strict but I could live with them.

When I arrived at the video link for my bail hearing Darren consulted with me in private beforehand. The goalposts had been shifted. The new female Investigating Officer had come on the scene and insisted on all sorts of draconian conditions. They were the strictest conditions ever in the UK. Let's not forget I was only charged in relation to unnotified public processions. Even the laughable Section 46 of the Serious Crime Act charges cited an unnotified procession as the 'crime' I was encouraging.

I could never work out this woman's agenda. Instead of just doing her job she had to try and persecute me. I can't grasp why. I have seen her in Court many times since and she seems to have a deep bitterness towards me. Perhaps it was a power thing and she wanted to feel that she was the one who would keep Jamie Bryson under wraps: the tough copper who could deal with this wee upstart loyalist. If that was her agenda then she failed miserably. I ended up pitying her. She used up so much of her energy on trying to persecute me.

Nevertheless I am glad she took charge of my case. I preferred someone full of bitterness and hatred. She was easy to draw out into silly squabbles. Week after week I put in bail variations and without fail she came up with outrageous objections. This kept the case constantly in the media and kept up the PSNIs humiliation. It was propaganda that you couldn't have paid for. An officer with more brains would have just acceded too many of my bail variation requests and approved them without going to Court. They would have then starved me of publicity for my case. Luckily for me I was up against an officer who played the tune every time I called it. She thought she was taking the hard line, the unbending copper. She was really feeding the propaganda machine that kept highlighting the farcical nature of my case.

Having an officer so hell bent on silencing me at any cost was ideal and it provided me with the perfect example to show people just how much the PSNI wanted to silence any political dissenters. She thought I was the fool: in reality she was being played like a fiddle from day one.

I finally received bail with the following conditions:

- Reside at (redacted for personal security reasons) and at no other address.
- Electronically tagged.
- Placed under curfew at (address redacted for personal security reasons) from the hours of 8pm until 7am.
- Forbidden from making any public speech or addressing any group of 3 or more people.
- Not to be within 4 miles of Belfast City Centre.
- Sign Bail 7 days a week.
- Not to use, have use of or be in possession of any mobile telephone or communication device.
- Not to wear clothing in any way that would conceal your identity.
- Not to make any public social media comment in relation to the Union Flag or any other protest.
- Not to participate in any public or media interview in relation to the Union Flag dispute or any other protest.
- Not to be within 1 mile of any public protest, demonstration or gathering.
- Not to be within 1 mile of any public procession, lawful or otherwise.
- Not to be in possession of, have use of or encourage anyone to communicate on your behalf via any electronic computer or device.

I was glad to be heading home. Stoner gave me a fantastic painting. I gave it straight to Tatty on the understanding he would never sell it. Picked up late in the afternoon, I enjoyed the drive home, stopping of in Kilcooley to call into Esther's on my way to Donaghadee. It was fantastic to see her. We had quite a lot to talk about but right now I was just glad to be out of prison.

On the night I came home I had many visitors. The UPF committee all came to visit. There was much that needed discussed. I made many good friends through the protest. Good loyal women made up a big part of the UPF committee. My friendship with some of those people faded slightly due to some disagreements. I really regret it came to that. They are good people, the salt of the earth and the backbone of loyalism. I will never forget their kindness and unwavering support during the protest. I hope that someday in the future we can rekindle the friendship that was forged over many cold nights and long road trips across the province.

I am hard work, very strong headed, and sometimes I could do with just listening to others and their viewpoints. That is one of my downfalls. I tend to try and do things my way. That isn't always compatible with building broad political movements.

There isn't a lot I would do differently but one thing I should have done more of was to listen to the viewpoints of those around me. To build any successful political movement or campaign requires people behind you who have a stake and an input into the direction of the movement. Howard Wells, the former CEO of the IFA once told me that the key to building anything successful is to surround yourself with people that can do things better than you can do them yourself. There were good people in the Ulster Peoples Forum, good people who never got an input into the direction of the group.

I genuinely believed in all of the decisions we made. Rightly or wrongly, sometimes you have to just make decisions and hope they turn out the way you want them to. In hindsight wider consultation and bringing more people on board would have been more beneficial. I did the best I could under the circumstances, and I hope I never forgot that the protests belonged to the people because it was those people who made me who I am today. Many of them trusted me to speak for them and I hope that I articulated their viewpoints and gave them a voice.

Sometimes I felt myself developing an ego and I didn't like it. I have to be honest in saying that. I did find it hard to keep my feet on the ground. I was thrust into the limelight and there were times I had to stop myself and say hold on, this isn't the Jamie Bryson show. I feel it's important to be open about that. I think everyone naturally has an ego that they want massaged. I would be a liar if I said there wasn't times that I behaved in an egotistical manner, of course there were. But it was very natural, a human reaction. All I ever wanted to do was what was right for our Country. That was the root and the base. I have learned that it is important to take stock sometimes and remind yourself what it is all about. You can get carried away easily.

I spent the days after I got out catching up with those within the protest movement. It seemed to me that there was a lack of direction and an absence of any coherent strategy. It seemed the PSNI had done what they set out to do. The weekly walks had ended. They ended days after I was arrested.

My bail conditions restricted me greatly but I did make an attempt to get the UPF going again. There was certainly the willingness within the group to move things forward. Sadly internal divisions began to appear. In hindsight I believe that maybe all the months of relentless pressure began to tell a bit and people just got weary. The UPF weren't getting as much media coverage. Since I had been arrested there wasn't really anyone who wanted to put their face out there, even through many were more than capable of articulating our viewpoints. I was banned from talking to the media, so John Wilson became the new Chairperson of the UPF.

It has been suggested that John Wilson never really existed, that he was a figure of imagination. It has been suggested that John Wilson was really just me using a cover name. It couldn't have been, because that would have been a breach of bail. And I wouldn't breach bail.

I wasn't allowed to communicate via any electronic device, internet or telephone. Some people think I was using a mobile phone that was kept down the side panel of my car from the day after I was released. But I couldn't have been, because the PSNI stopped and searched me regularly and I could never have outsmarted the PSNI. It would also have been a breach of bail. And I wouldn't breach bail.

I wasn't allowed to attend any protests of course. Someone said that I was at the Bangor protest at Bloomfield roundabout this year, the protest about the 12th parade in Ardoyne. It was even alleged that a photograph exists of me wearing glasses, a fake beard and hiding up a tree. But that would have been a breach of bail. And I wouldn't breach bail.

The Sunday Life carried a picture following the City Hall rally on the anniversary of the beginning of the flag protests. The picture showed a man wearing a Santa hat, a beard and glasses.

Fighting the Conditions

The bail conditions I was placed under were the most stringent possible. The female PSNI officer had insisted upon them being set, and she insisted on them remaining. I would still be on those conditions if she had her way.

I decided early on that the best way to challenge the conditions was to use their own system against them. I resolved to make a bail variation request every week. Winning new freedoms would be great; but if I didn't then it still kept my case highlighted and exposed the PSNI's oppressive attempts to silence me.

I requested to attend many contentious events. I did this because I knew that was the best way to draw the Investigating Officer out into making outrageous objections. It became a weekly pantomime. The person I felt sorry for was the PSNI Court liaison officer; she was a decent person to whom I came to like. She was only doing her job. Week in week out she was sent to the witness stand with a list of comical objections. While it made her look silly, it was the IO who was making all these objections and then this poor officer had to take to the witness stand trying and defend the indefensible.

The first variation I lodged was to attend the Ulster Volunteer Force centenary celebrations in East Belfast. This was to be a fantastic day and I thought the request was reasonable. The IO obviously didn't. The PSNI took to the stand and portrayed me as a dangerous terrorist, saying that with almost 12,000 people in attendance that if I went I could encourage all these people to become violent. It sounded ridiculous. One man out of 12,000 and suddenly the place was going to go into uproar. This is the kind of fantasy the PSNI indulged in.

Sadly many of the Judges bought their nonsense. The Judge that day was bombarded with an unbelievable amount of fantasy. He came down on the side of the PSNI and I was denied the right to attend. It has been said that I attended the night prior to the event to see Craigavon House but PSNI heard I was there and since it was only 3.7 miles from Belfast Centre instead of 4 miles, they were coming to arrest me. It was alleged I once again found myself in the boot of the car with the PSNI left scratching their heads. But I wouldn't have done that, because that would have been a breach of bail.

Jim Dowson was representing himself at this early stage of his case and he asked me to be his legal advisor. It's called a McKenzie friend in legal circles. I attended Court for Jim's first appearance after he got bail. The anger on the face of the IO was a sight to see. She was spitting nails, furious because by being at the Court I was within 4 miles of Belfast City Centre. However, the condition stated that I was permitted to attend Court; therefore on those occasions the 4 mile restriction was lifted. She argued that because I wasn't the subject of the Court hearing and my reason for being there was as Jim's legal advisor that this was not covered in my conditions and that I had broken bail. I told her to go ahead and breach me then. I hung the bait out for her hoping in her desperation she would take it and indeed bring me back before the Court. It would have been fantastic propaganda- "Your honour Mr Bryson was within 4 miles of Belfast City Centre, he was attending Court in an official capacity to assist a man without legal representation..."- but she didn't take the bait on this occasion.

A few months later my conditions were changed to not being within 500 yards of City Hall. This meant I could attend Court as often as I wanted, and indeed I did. I went and supported flag protestors and on one such occasion the IO from my case was in the Courtroom. She spotted me and began berating the Court liaison officer who had agreed to the change. She was furious; the anger on her face was something I will never forget. I don't smoke but that day I wished I had a big Cuban cigar to light up. It just went to show how personally involved in the case she was becoming. She got so worked up because I wasn't banned from being within 4 miles of Belfast City Centre, why? What was the necessity of this condition in the first place?

I was playing football for 1st Bangor FC and we were heading for promotion and had a couple of mid-week games to play. I lodged a variation with the Court to have my curfew extended by an hour until 9pm to allow me to play in these evening games. I thought this was reasonable but the PSNI objections that day were perhaps the most ridiculous to date. They objected to me being allowed out for an extra hour because I could influence others in the team. They really did say that, check the court records, it is there in black and white. They are so intelligent that they didn't realise that even if they got their way and I could only play the first half, I still could have used this 'influence' they spoke about during the first 45 minutes. I am still not sure what influence I could have exerted over my football team mind you, it was simply comical. They said they had to maintain public order; yet they have never been able to explain to me how there would have been even the remotest threat to public order by allowing me to play a football match in Newtownards.

My Barrister didn't even have to speak. The Judge tore the PSNI apart and the expression on their face was priceless. The Judge knew this was simply farcical. It became a running joke in the football team that we couldn't take a short corner because if two of us gathered around the flag and then moved into the box the PSNI IO would say I held a flag protest and then organised a procession. Her hatred provided us with much comedy in the changing room. We did get promoted. It was a great achievement for the boys. I missed most of the games from December to April so it wasn't really my achievement. I only played a small role at the beginning and the end, but it was a great time at the club.

The fight in the Courtroom began to intensify. Few Magistrates cases last beyond 6 months. But unsurprisingly mine was trundling on. The PPS refused to confirm if they were proceeding with the Serious Crime Charges, and said they had to examine my computers. First the PPS told the Judge this was being done. That bought them 6 weeks. Then after 6 weeks they told the Judge they made a mistake, the computers hadn't even been sent off to be looked at it. They didn't make a mistake; they lied. The funny thing about the computers was that they weren't even mine: they belonged to Tatty.

It was a joke. They abused the process so as to enable them to drag the Serious Crime Act charges of encouraging an unnotified public procession out for as long as they could. Given that section 46 was designed for encouraging serious violent offences and terrorism, it was preposterous that the PSNI and PPS even pretended they were going to proceed for encouraging a procession.

The marching season was approaching and so far the PSNI IO was objecting to everything and anything. I indentified the 1 of July Remembrance parade as a key battleground. I thought that the PSNI IO would be daft enough to bite, and this time she did. The 1 July Remembrance parade in Bangor is a yearly event which includes a religious service and parade. I always lay a wreath on behalf of our band, the Bangor Protestant Boys. I reckoned that the IO would object and box herself into a corner. It was one thing objecting to attending a run of the mill parade, it was quite another when you were trying to stop a man remembering his war dead. The IO was blinded to the fact that she was being lured into a trap. I decided that on this issue I would make a stand. I would be attending and laying the wreath and if the PSNI wanted to arrest me for that then so be it.

Local political figures were outraged and local PSNI commanders began to realise the potential for a public relations nightmare if they were forced to take action against me. Privately the local PSNI made it known to political representatives that they had no objections to me attending and could not see the logic in the IO's objections. But she stood firm and refused to budge. I let it be known that I would be attending the parade regardless of what the PSNI or the court said and this ended up being widely covered in the media, which ratcheted up the tension no end. The PSNI were trapped in a catch 22 situation. If it was a game of chess it was checkmate. Blinded by her hatred towards me and her desire to suppress every human right I had, the IO in the case couldn't see that she was being led up the garden path. A wiser officer would have spotted the bear trap from the beginning and simply agreed for me to attend, thus avoiding the wagons circling around them.

The Magistrates Court was afraid to make a decision on it. The Judge said no but interestingly she said we could appeal. She made a point of saying that, which was unusual. The scene was set for Belfast High court, a hearing in front of Justice Weir, one of Northern Irelands most experienced and senior judges.

The night before the hearing there was an attempt to remove my legal aid. Apparently it was not in the public interest that I have this High Court hearing. I told my solicitor to go back and tell them that I would simply represent myself in the High court. They quickly re-instated the legal aid. I don't think anyone relished the thought of giving me such a platform in front of the media.

Prior to the hearing my legal team came out and said the PSNI had backed down and wanted to make a deal. I could attend the religious part of the ceremony only, in plain clothes. I knew then I had won. They had to come and offer a deal. I told them they could stick their deal up their arse. Just who do they think they are? I will remember our fallen in whichever way I see fit- I certainly wasn't going to beg the PSNI for the right. No deal.

The hearing began and the PPS Barrister- the one who had spewed so much hatred at my High Court bail hearing- had hardly began speaking when Justice Weir got tore into her demanding to know why the PSNI were banning people from public processions? Surely that was the job of the Parades Commission he said. The PPS representative began to get flustered and repeatedly asked Justice Weir if he wanted to hear about my charges. He shot back that he did not and in a classic put down he said *"I have a television like everyone else, so no I do not need you to give me any background to the charges."* I was enjoying this hearing more than any previously. I was praying that it would continue and continue it did.

The PSNI then whispered in the ear of the PPS who said that didn't mind me attending the ceremony, but no parade and no band uniform. Justice Weir said that he was going to allow me to go and could see no logical reason why the PSNI and PPS were still trying to ban me from the parade. He had made quite clear that he was not willing to do that. In desperate fashion the PPS then almost begged the Judge. They begged for him to ban me from wearing my band uniform. The Judge dismissed them. My Barrister didn't even have to open his mouth. They had hung themselves with their own rope.

Try for just one minute to find any reason why the PSNI were so obsessed with me being banned from even wearing a band uniform?

There is no logical reason for this. My only conclusion is that the IO was waging a personal vendetta against me and that all these objections were little more than her trying to oppress me as much as was humanly possible. It was a good thing mind you because a smarter PSNI officer would have been much more difficult to go up against. This IO was quite obviously emotionally involved in the case therefore the political agenda was easy to expose. I just had to dangle the red flag and the PSNI came charging.

The case progressed as slowly as the PPS could manage. Everyone knew the serious crime charges would be dropped, they couldn't proceed. They would have been lucky to find a judge to even hear those charges due to the fact they were that ludicrous. They would have been laughed out of court and well they know it. I believe the PSNI desperately wanted the stringent bail conditions to be kept on me and for this reason they pressured the PPS into dragging the case out. They went on that long that it got to the stage that it became embarrassing for them.

Finally they ran out of road with the serious crime charges. They contacted Darren and told him they would be withdrawing them. I announced this on social media and the UPF released a press statement.

The PPS and PSNI were furious; they felt this was rubbing their noses in it. But why shouldn't I rub their noses in it? After all they had done on me they expected me to afford them some kind of respect and take some kind of oath never to expose what they had done? I don't think so. I have no respect for them whatsoever.

If I have embarrassed them then I am happy enough about that, I hope this book embarrasses them and causes them to have many questions to answer about their conduct. It is no more than they so richly deserve.

The PPS came to court a few days later and decided they would not be dropping the serious crime charges. They even began to suggest that they could run the 'taking part in an unnotified procession' charges in the Magistrates court and run the serious crime charges of 'encouraging an unnotified procession' in the Crown court. This bizarre suggestion has no legal precedent; once again they just tried to make the rules up as they went along.

It was comical when they began to realise that the serious crime charges could only be dealt with by a Crown court but that the unnotified public procession charges could only be dealt with by a Magistrates court. They effectively had charged me with a summary only offence that could only be tried by indictment. It began to look in danger of being exposed as the major cock up that it so evidently was.

To try and buy them some time the prosecutor stood up in the court and told the Judge that the DPP had to personally review the charges because the case had a high profile. The judge asked why, he said he had never heard of this before. The prosecutor said that this was internal PPS guidelines and that any case with a high profile had to be referred to the director for the final decision. This was a lot of nonsense and I knew it.

I sent an FOI to the PPS. They had to respond and admit no such guidelines existed and thus they were condemned as liars by their own words. The FOI is included at the end of this chapter.

Soon it started to be raised in court about the legality of using section 46 legislation- which could only be tried by indictment- whilst the offence allegedly being encouraged is a summary only matter. The PPS buckled. They didn't want that being aired in a public courtroom. They dropped the charges.

They were always dropping the charges. In my mind they would have already told the PSNI that the charges would never stick prior to my arrest. They only acceded to playing the game so as to allow the PSNI to have me placed on stringent bail conditions and remanded in custody. They effectively abused the process of law to give the PSNI a political weapon.

The day after my serious crime charges were dropped I made an application to have all the bail conditions relating to speaking to the media, using social media and computers etc removed. There was no lawful justification to have them there. How could a man be banned from talking to the media because he had been charged with an unnotified public procession?

The PSNI just couldn't take their medicine. They couldn't accept that this particular phase of their political campaign against me had ended. They wanted the bail conditions to stay.

Judge Fiona Bagnall heard the bail variation hearing. The PSNI provided perhaps their most ridiculous and desperate performance yet. The Judge asked them how they expected her to justify restricting my freedom of speech given that no relevant charges existed. The PSNI said they felt I would have a destabilising effect on an already delicate political situation. The Judge informed the PSNI that they seemed to misunderstand her role- she was not there to manage politics or society- she was there to make Judgements within the law and continuing with such conditions had no legal basis. The Judge said that she could not understand why the PSNI were so keen to have these conditions imposed.

Let's not forget the PSNI are supposed to be non political and here they were trying to meddle in politics, using the law to suppress political dissent. The Judge said she couldn't accept any of the PSNI objections as legitimate. She asked if they had anything else relevant or sensible to say, the PSNI said that they wanted me banned from social media- the Judge asked why- the PSNI answered- *"well your honour, because he has well over 5,000 followers on twitter."*

The courtroom exploded with howls of laughter. It was like stand up comedy. The Judge digested the comments for a minute and then said she had heard enough. She handed over to my barrister to cross examine in the PSNI.

The Judge halted the cross examination after exactly 27 seconds. It was a massacre. The Judge saved the PSNI from any further embarrassment. I don't know why, I wish she had of let them continue, it had the potential for a great reality TV show- PSNI courtroom comedy!

With the bail conditions removed I was free to speak to the media. Stephen Nolan got in touch to see if I would be interested in doing an interview on his show the following morning. I was more than happy to oblige.

I always found Stephen a decent person. He is a lot different away from the camera. He has a job to do. He is in essence an entertainer- an actor - and he acts his role well. When you speak to him personally, away from cameras and microphones, he is great craic and I have to say I have a lot of time for him.

I did the interview with Stephen the following morning. It was about 25 minutes long and covered a wide range of issues. I wanted to try and explain to the public- in simple terms- the complex nature of my case. I wanted to ensure people understood just how laughable the whole thing was.

Stephen raised a very significant point. He said that he could not grasp how the PSNI and PPS were able to say there was sufficient evidence to charge me, and then all of a sudden there was insufficient evidence when it got to the stage of actually having to produce it in a courtroom.

The PSNI will contrive charges against anyone who they view as a threat to the political stability of the so called peace process. Then aided and abetted by the PPS they will try to have the person remanded or politically restricted with outrageous bail conditions.

Whilst continuing to fight the conditions and unable to speak in public I was subjected to a hate campaign by some elements of the media. Fictional stories appeared almost weekly. These stories were designed to discredit and try and make a mockery of me.

I have a pretty decent relationship with some of the media. I think the likes of Allison Morris, Suzanne Breen and Sara Girvin are good journalists. If they are running a story about me they always have the decency to give me a call and ask for my side of it. I don't mind that. They have a job to do as well.

There was a story in the Sunday World- that rag of a paper- that claimed my uncle was an IRA commander called Jim Bryson. That was completely and utterly false. It just simply had no basis in reality, yet the Sunday World still ran the story.

They knew full well they had lied and printed a false story. They apologised a few weeks later. The apology said sorry to the family of Jim Bryson- the IRA commander- for falsely saying he was related to me. That shows you the kind of people working for that rag of a paper- they couldn't find it in them to apologise to me for linking me with a despicable IRA terrorist- instead they apologised for linking the terrorist to me.

The Sunday Life also ran the fairytale about me ordering an Indian curry. It was a disgraceful story. The Jim Bryson story and the Indian curry story are really the only two times I have been furious about what has been printed about me. Most opinions and viewpoints- especially those written by clowns trying to fill column inches- just go over my head. But those two stories were deliberate lies designed to discredit me.

The Sunday World later claimed they had run an investigation and 'uncovered' that I was doing the double. Again this was totally false. They claimed I was working as a taxi operator and at the same time claiming job seekers allowance. They wanted to paint me as some kind of low life dole cheat.

The truth is that I was actually working along with Kare Kabs on a voluntary community project. I was seeing if they could design an employment scheme for young people within the local area. They genuinely wanted to do something positive in the community, and they ended up having their business plastered all over the front page of a Sunday rag by some pathetic excuse for a journalist. Their 'crime' was having me in their office to try and draw up a scheme to bring young people into employment.

I wasn't a dole cheat. There was never any allegation from the dole that I had cheated by doing any paid work in Kare Kabs. The Sunday World made that up; they concocted a deliberate lie, nothing new there. Kare Kabs as a business suffered adversely because they tried to do something positive.

The PSNI raided the premises- they didn't even have the correct address on the warrant- the warrant was addressed to the community office of the Voluntary Education Forum.

The PSNI also visited Kare Kabs and asked the manager what I was doing there? They told her I was a bad person and that they should be careful having me around the place. It was that same clown that arrested me. He really thinks he is something that guy, the self styled sheriff. It is none of his business what I was doing there and what right did he think he had to go in an express his personal viewpoint on me?

I worked every day since I left school up until I was maliciously arrested. I am not some lay-about that doesn't want to work. I lost my job when I was arrested by the PSNI and when I was released could anyone logically tell me it would have been beneficial for me to work?

There is no use in me trying to be all moralistic about it: the fact is that if I worked, then I would be working to pay legal fees to defend myself against a politically contrived and maliciously concocted case. They have dragged the case out for two years and I have spent much of those two years in the High Court. If I was working then every single penny I had- and more- would have went on paying legal fees. Why should I? I did nothing wrong.

The harsh truth is that I didn't work whilst on bail because I wasn't working to pay legal fees; especially not legal fees for a case where I have been made a political scapegoat. The system conspired against me because my political viewpoint didn't suit. So I worked the system back on them. All is fair in love and war!

As the case became more of a circus, we decided to play along. Willie Frazer and I dressed up to go to Court. Willie dressed as Abu Hamza- a real Islamist hate preacher- and I wore a wig and taped my mouth up to symbolise the attack on free speech being carried out by the PSNI and PPS.

It must be remembered that the PSNI actually made an application to have Willie and me banned from all media. Thankfully the Judge realised that this would be so extreme that she couldn't possibly justify it and she denied their application.

The Judge eventually lifted all the restrictions on my free speech. It had been a long road but I fought them every step of the way.

Some people would say the conditions were worthless because I managed to circumvent them all in one way or another, but I couldn't possibly comment on that, you would need to ask John Wilson!

FOI response from PPS

This FOI proves that the PPS used legislation against me that had NEVER before been used for a summary only offence.
It also proves that the PPS Barrister that told the Judge during my case that the PPS taking so long to make a decision whether to continue with my prosecution or not because "high profile cases have to go to the DPP for a decision" was telling a blatant lie. No such internal guidelines exist.

Mr Jamie Bryson
Email: jamiebryson@ymail.com

04th November 2013

Our Ref: FOI request 13/356

Dear Mr. Bryson

I refer to your email dated 08th October 2013 in which you asked for several pieces of information. This request has been dealt with under the terms of the Freedom of Information Act 2000.

Freedom of Information Act 2000

The Freedom of Information Act creates rights of access for any person making a request for information to a public authority. The rights of access are twofold. First, to be informed by the public authority if it holds information of the description specified in the request, and if that is the case, secondly, to be provided with that information. These rights are subject to important limitations, which are designed to achieve a proper balance between the right to know and considerations of law and policy in the broader public interest.

You had asked the following: (1) since the passing of the Serious Crime Act 2007 how many people within N.Ireland have been charged with Indictable only Section 46 when the alleged 'encouraging' offence was a summary only matter?

In total, seven suspects have been issued with an indictable prosecution decision for offences under Section 46 of the Serious Crime Act 2007. One of these suspects was prosecuted for 'Encouraging or assisting assault believing one or more will be committed' which is an indictable offence and is tried at the Crown Court. The remaining 6 suspects were prosecuted for 'Encouraging or assisting offences believing one or more will be committed' which is a hybrid offence and may be tried at either the Magistrates' or Crown Court. Please note that for hybrid offences, on taking a decision to prosecute, the Public Prosecutor must also decide whether the defendant should be tried in the Magistrates' Court or the Crown Court. In making this decision the prosecutor will consider whether the Magistrates' Court is the appropriate venue in that it has sufficient sentencing powers in relation to the gravity of the offence.

No summary prosecution decisions have ever been issued for offences under Section 46 of the Serious Crime Act 2007 and two suspects have received no prosecution decisions.

(2) In how many instances since 2011 have the PPS separated a case file, for example running a trial in a Magistrate's and Crown court?

With regard to question 2, I can inform you that the PPS Case Management System does not hold the information requested in a form from which it can be readily extracted. To answer your request would require a manual search. This would easily exceed the cost limit as defined in Section 12 of the Act which makes provision for public authorities to refuse requests for information where the cost of dealing with them would exceed the appropriate limit, for the PPS as a Government Department the limit is set at £600. This represents the estimated cost of one person spending 3.5 working days in determining whether the department holds the information, locating, retrieving and extracting the information.

(3) Could I please receive a copy of the 'Internal best practice guidelines' that stipulates for any case with 'media attention that the Director must personally make the charging decision'. (This was stated by PPS representative in Belfast Magistrates Court)

(4) In conjunction with Q3 could I please have a copy of the guidelines for deciding if a case has sufficient media attention to warrant invoking the 'best practice guidelines' and referring to the Director.

(5) Can I please have referenced the training procedures undertaken by Case officers that is relevant to how they differentiate between cases and whether they can or cannot make a charging decision based on 'media attention'.

(6) In conjunction with Q5 could I also have referenced where within the PPS legislative remit it defines how much 'media attention' requires a case to be referred to the Director for charging decision.

With regard to questions 3, 4, 5 and 6, I can advise that in general terms cases which attract press and media attention may be drawn to the attention of the Director's Private Office. This is because the Director's Private Office receives enquiries from the media, public and public representatives about cases which are attracting attention.
I can however confirm that there is no such written PPS policy or guidelines stipulating when and if cases attracting media attention should be referred. Therefore in terms of Section 17 of the FOI Act the information you requested is not held.

If you are dissatisfied in any way with the handling of your request, you have the right to request a review in accordance with our review procedure. Alternatively, you may wish to apply directly to the Information Commissioner for a decision.

Yours Sincerely, PPS FOI Section

The Case Continues

When the serious crime charges were withdrawn you could be forgiven for thinking it was all systems go, full steam ahead to the trial for the remaining 5 charges. Four counts of an unnotified public procession and one count of wilfully obstructing a public highway. The PSNI had all the evidence when they arrested me, so why over a year later had the case still not been listed for trial?

I began to request disclosure from the PSNI about the meetings they held during the flag protests. Much of this is covered in the later chapter relating to the Ulster People's Forum. The meetings were relevant because the PSNI agreed to facilitate the weekly walks and then further on down the line arrested, remanded and then placed outrageous bail conditions on me for taking part in them. They were the ones that told me it was legal.

The PSNI cannot be trusted. I have no time for them whatsoever. I believe they are politically compromised. If you did a survey on the middle management of the PSNI, those who run the organisation on a day to day basis, you would surely find most of the posts are occupied by Roman Catholics. Old school RUC officers with much more experience and wisdom are overlooked for these posts in favour of the post Patten generation of PSNI officers. It is shameful really. Most former RUC officers I speak to despise what the PSNI has become.

The PSNI initially refused to hand over the disclosure relevant to the case. They cited National Security in an FOI response to me. What was the National Security issue? I think that it's a lot of bollocks. The truth is that we had them over a barrel and they tried to hide behind National Security to prevent them having to reveal the fact that they sat in meetings and agreed to facilitate what they later termed to be illegal. The PPS knew this and played along with it.

I was fast losing patience with the PPS; the new prosecutor was a middle aged man with some kind of beard. He was a jumped up little character, full of beans and arrogance. I kept reminding myself that one day this clown would be asking me questions, trying to grill me on the stand and I knew I would make an idiot of him. I am sure the man is not an idiot. In fact I am sure he is pretty intelligent, but he was behaving like an idiot. He was eventually removed from the case and replaced by a senior barrister.

Strangely enough I was instantly impressed with the new prosecutor. He carried himself well and acted like a consummate professional who was just there to do his job. I don't mind that. I respect it. No personal agenda, no hatred seeping from his pores, no attempts to play dirty tricks. He gave me the impression he was fair. He was the complete opposite from the original prosecutor, a spiteful little man who was constantly yakking away like an annoying bird.

The PPS continued to object to handing over the disclosure of the meetings. At one review hearing the prosecutor stood up and said that he didn't think it was relevant and that the PSNI had told those at the meeting the weekly walks were illegal. That was a blatant lie so I stood up from the public gallery and said "your honour, that man is a liar" the judge told me to be quite but I repeated my allegation. I stand over it to this day. The PPS and PSNI told lies, blatant lies and malicious lies. That shouldn't shock people, they do it quite regularly.

On another occasion the IO in my case was on the stand. Whatever it was she was talking about caused us to explode into howls of laughter. It was farcical. The judge said if we didn't like what was going on we could leave. I stood up and said that given her invitation I would have to leave, because the whole thing was a complete and utter circus. The officer on the stand was quite obviously performing the clown act. She shot a glare towards me, one of those thousand yard stares that the WWE wrestlers do to keep the kids entertained. I don't know whether she thought it would have any effect or not, she could still be staring for all I care.

The case maintained an unbelievably pedestrian pace. The PPS and the PSNI used every opportunity they could get to have it adjourned and delayed. I think they liked the idea of keeping me under some kind of bail conditions. Maybe it makes them feel important. I think it does, but I think there is a much wider political agenda at play.

Suddenly there was a break in the case. Out of the blue all charges were dropped against Willie Frazer. Every man and their dog then believed that my charges would naturally be dropped as well. After all we walked in the same so-called processions, side by side and the evidence against u s was identical. Exactly the same video evidence was being used in the two cases yet the PPS and PSNI drop one and proceed with the other? That requires an explanation. Even Willie has himself expressed shock and disbelief. There is a clear disparity in the handling of the two cases.

Not long after Willie's charges were dropped I received a legal letter from a private firm acting on behalf of Barra McGrory QC, the DPP. They demanded the removal of tweets and comments I had made, many of which exposed the DPP's past links to members of the IRA Army Council. I had repeatedly alleged that the DPP had represented IRA members who had been involved in a secret deal with the Government, I was proved right. Barra McGrory was the solicitor that acting corporately on behalf of the IRA OTR's. I had raised this matter and Mr McGrory's involvement in the OTR scheme for quite some time; I submitted documents to MP's on the NI Select Affairs Committee and following this they asked a number of questions of the DPP (various extracts are included in the books appendix). In answer to one of the questions Barra McGrory clearly states that his only role in the OTR scheme was to "submit names" and that he only had some brief engagement in 1999. Interestingly however the Hallett review- commissioned by the Government- states that Mr McGrory took part in meetings in 2006. So just what exactly is the truth?

Here are extracts from both the NI Select Affairs Committee and the Hallett report which clearly show the conflicting accounts of our current DPP's involvement in the OTR scheme:

(NI Select Affairs Committee 10th June 2014)

Q1357 Kate Hoey: Yes, but the letter is actually saying—you have seen the letter, so presumably you have seen the wording of some of the letters. They are different wordings, we understand.

Barra McGrory: I have since I became Director of Public Prosecutions. My role in private practice, apart from some engagement with Peter Sheridan and the Attorney-General's office back in 1999, was simply to submit names. I never saw the letters at that time, but I have seen them now.

(Hallett review- Meeting of 9 June 2006)

"This led to a further meeting (at which ACC Sheridan was present) with Barra McGrory, a lawyer who acted for Sinn Fein (and was appointed Director of Public Prosecutions for Northern Ireland in 2011). At a meeting on 7 December 2006 with the Legal Services Branch of the PSNI, Mr

McGrory discussed various possible ways in which OTRs could have their cases considered."

From the above extracts the question must clearly be asked, why does the Hallett report say Mr McGrory attended meetings in 2006 and discussed the ways the OTR scheme could operate whilst he himself told the NI Select Affairs committee that he simply submitted names?

I refused to remove the tweets and comments. I still haven't. I sent word back that Barra could sue me if he wanted. I would welcome it. I could then expose the sordid deal that is the Hillsborough Agreement in a public courtroom. I am still waiting. The letter from the DPP's solicitors is included in the appendix of this book along with my response to it.

What is interesting is that the DPP used public money from the PPS funds to pay a private legal firm to try and silence me. Yet another gross abuse of process. The confirmation that the DPP used public money to employ a private legal firm to shut me up is also included in the appendix of this book. Kate Hoey MP challenged Mr McGrory about his attempts to have my twitter account shut down during the hearing being held by the NI Select Affairs committee. Here is the extract from the minutes of that meeting:

Q1434 Kate Hoey: Do you think it is sensible and just for your department to be pursuing—presumably at public expense—the Twitter account of one particular resident in Northern Ireland, because they have been saying certain things that may not necessarily be very nice about you?

Barra McGrory: The things that that individual has said about me are not just not nice, but grossly defamatory. They allege that I am personally a terrorist. They damage the administration of justice in this jurisdiction and they damage the office of Director of
Public Prosecutions and I make no apology for any action I have taken in respect of that.

Kate Hoey: We'll see. Thank you.

The PPS and the PSNI were finally forced to hand over disclosure of the meetings that had taken place, and here came another bombshell. The names of the three men who had met the Chief Constable the night prior to me arrest were there in black and white:

Gerry Kelly (the old bailey former) Martin McGuinness (the former IRA chief of staff) and Sean 'spike' Murray (the IRA man who had recently been exposed by BBC Spotlight for gunrunning during the so called peace process.

The fact that these three sat down and discussed me-and the wider Union flag protests- with the Chief Constable and he danced straightaway to their tune straightaway is highly significant. It shows the political nature of the PSNI, it just goes to show how much political influence republicans can exert over the PSNI. It is shameful and it is walking on the graves of the RUC men and women who gave their lives fighting the IRA. The PSNI are now mere political puppets of the IRA's alter ego, Sinn Fein.

Sinn Fein had been agitating to have me arrested for weeks. Alex Maskey began laying the ground on the Nolan Show a couple of weeks prior to my arrest. I met Maskey outside Stormont last year and had a conversation with him. I told him how I felt the justice system was being abused and I asked him if he thought that was fair and if that was the shared society Sinn Fein spoke of. He agreed my case was a farce and said he would raise the issue. He never bothered. Then again, why would he? I am an opponent of Sinn Fein. They are no friends of mine.

I met Peter Robinson in his office at Stormont around this time. A local MLA had signalled to me that Peter wanted to see if we could improve relationships for the betterment of Unionism. I said I would be willing to hear what he had to say.

I went to Stormont and spent over an hour with Peter. I did make clear to him that I opposed Peter Robinson the politician but I didn't know Peter Robinson the person so it wasn't personal. I never quite got where he was coming from. I got the feeling that Peter felt it would be much better for the DUP if they could get me onside. That was never likely to happen. He did ask me to join the DUP. That was never likely to happen either.

There was nothing heated at the meeting, it was relaxed and cordial. He is an intelligent man, a political survivor. His special advisor Timothy Johnston was there but I didn't make much of him. The last time I had been at a meeting with Peter Robinson at Stormont, it was over a row in North Down in relation to the Council's handling of PEACE 3 money. Emma Little was there with Peter that day. She seemed a wee bit more intelligent and switched on (formerly I think she was a barrister).

I went on holiday at the start of July expecting my case to finally be heard on the 16 of July. I returned to the news that it had been delayed. The PPS were once again refusing to hand over documentation relevant to the case. Nothing shocked me anymore.

During this period I began to be lambasted day and daily by one particular social media account which seemed to know a hell of a lot about the internal workings of my case. I let this play out for a few weeks before contacting the account and putting it to them that I believed the person behind this account was actually an officer involved in my case. The account initially denied all knowledge but when I made it known that the Ombudsman could end up investigating, there was a sudden revelation that the person behind this account was a friend of one of the officers in my case. Or so they said. I decided to play along with this, certain that the name used by the account was false and it was more than likely the officer operating it.

I couldn't believe the lengths these people would go it. It became a running joke; I toyed with them a bit, feeding them straight lines here and there. I came to pity it all. If I really wanted to I could refer it to the Ombudsman and have them investigate if indeed a PSNI officer had been trolling a suspect in a case they were handling, but what would be the point. If that is the case then I feel sorry for the officer. They must be consumed with hatred for me. What a sad way to life your life.

On 8 October 2014 my contest was scheduled to go ahead. Once again I had deliberately upped the ante prior to the case. There was no way I was going to let it quietly pass as the PSNI and PPS wanted. Why should I? I deserve my day on the stand. I deserve to tell my side of the story and be able to defend myself.

The support I had at the court was quite amazing. My case was moved to a smaller courtroom, presumably to restrict many of my supporters from attending. The hallway, public gallery and foyer were rammed full of supporters. The authorities didn't like that.

One of the officers who was there as a 'witness', knows a friend of mine. He remarked to him that this was the biggest load of crap and he had been called in to be briefed about it at 8am. They were leaving no stone unturned in their quest to have me convicted.

Prior to the start of the hearing my legal team asked for a consultation with me and they made me aware that- quite amazingly- the PPS had decided to try and shift the goalposts at the last minute.

The basis of British law is that every man is innocent until proven guilty. It is a fundamental right in the ECHR Article 6 that the duty is on the State to prove **beyond all reasonable doubt** the guilt of the accused. This means that if there is even the slightest doubt in the judge's mind then the accused should be acquitted of the charges.

The PPS have attempted to flip all this on its head, entirely in contravention of Article 6 of ECHR. They asked the court to put the burden of proof onto the defence, effectively meaning that the Crown would only have to prove I was guilty on the balance of probabilities whilst I would have to prove I was not guilty beyond all reasonable doubt.

They sought to entirely reverse the principle of innocent until proven guilty that had stood from the days of the Magna Carta. It was shocking. Even by the standards of these people it was shocking. They hoped my legal team would just accept this change and therefore it would be madness for me to take the stand as I would almost condemn myself. They didn't want me on the stand and this was their final throw of the dice to try and prevent it. They are scared of what I have to say, they don't want Pandora's Box being opened.

My legal team refused to accept this farcical attempt to usurp my basic human rights. The judge refused to make a ruling and asked for a full hearing on this particular legal point. If the PPS got away with this it would mean anyone on parade-related charges wouldn't stand a chance. It would be impossible to put up a reasonable defence. It is an attempt by the PPS to circumvent the basic principle of a fair trial. If they get away with this it will effectively give the PSNI & the PPS the ability to convict everyone of any parade related offence without the person having a fair trial or any reasonable defence. It is an attempt to plug the gap. To protect the PSNI from scrutiny for their actions and their facilitation of parades which they say at the time is legal and then months down the line say it was actually illegal and proceed to prosecute the people who took part.

I will not be bowing down to them. If I accept this just to get things over and done with it will have much wider ramifications for all protests and parades. It will provide a legal precedent. I will not accept that. I have fought them every step of the way and I will continue to fight them every step of the way... to the House of Lords and on to the European Court of

Human Rights if need be. Trust me, if it is a battle of wills they will lose hands down.

What they can't understand is that they are paid Government puppets who are fighting me just because they have been told to. They are paid to fight me. I volunteer to fight them for love of my Country. This simple fact makes it impossible for them to win.

Some men can't be bought, bullied or talked around. I am one of them. If you want to shut me up then you have only one option- put a bullet in the back of my head. Even then, I still win as you are only sending me to be with my God!

Welcome to Loyalist North Down

A few years prior to the start of the widespread Union flag protests there was a highly contentious protest that took place Bangor, the area dubbed the Gold coast.

This protest came about because of North Down Borough Councils lack of respect for Protestant, Unionist and Loyalist culture. They treated loyalists with contempt and referred to our Union flag as a 'rag'.

The row initially erupted because certain members of the council had proposed fining local bonfire committees because there were too many flags flying. I could never understand these people.

There are some decent Councillors in North Down but the vast majority were and remain complete and utter muppets. Middle class snobs who wish they could take every working class estate in the area and wheel it up to Belfast, away from their precious Gold coast. I expect that attitude from those in the Alliance party etc, but the attitude of some of the so called Unionists towards local loyalists is contemptuous. They forget that it is loyalists who would have to do their fighting for them if conflict broke out tomorrow. They would be hiding under the bed, occasionally posing for a picture in the local paper.

Many of these idiots are surrounded by blind sheep. Some local DUP members and their hangers on near had a nervous breakdown because local bands stood for more than 3 minutes as part of the 12th July 'graduated response'. As I have alluded to earlier in the book, the graduated response was more of a graduated surrender. The biggest pile of shite I have ever heard.

This protest- in 2009- began by erecting flags all around the Borough. The protest targeted the most affluent areas and thus achieved maximum publicity.

The great and the good were doing well out of the peace process, they despised the sight of flags. They despised the flag of their own Country. In my mind they are selfish snobs who would happily sell their Country as long as they still got their fat pay cheques at the end of the month. All they want is to have a bulging bank account and be able to close their curtains and watch Coronation Street every night.

I played an active role from the very beginning. For four weeks we ran the PSNI ragged, they were chasing their tail and the beauty of the whole thing was that everything we did was totally within the law.

They tried to stop us putting up flags and congregating in groups because they said it could constitute a breach of the peace. We drew up a constitution and became the official lamppost spotting society. There was bemusement on the PSNI Sergeants face when he turned up and demanded we moved on, but then he was presented with a copy of our constitution which gave us justification for our presence in the area. There was nothing he could do but watch on in amazement.

The erection of flags continued for weeks and the NIO became involved. They decided to convene round table talks to try and address the issues. I was one of a number of community workers invited. They were paying us lip service, anything to keep the peace. The PSNI just wanted an end to the protest because it was tying up so much of their resources. The NIO wanted political stability, the last thing they needed was this spreading (little did they know that North Down in 2009 was only the birth pangs, it would be 3 years later on the 3rd December 2012 when the volcano really erupted). I thought the talks were a waste of time, the Council promised all sorts, but within 12 months they would renege on all of that.

The erection of flags phase of the protest ended following the round table talks. It was agreed to give them a chance to see what they could come up with, some wanted to give them the benefit of the doubt.

A few months down the line they began to renege on their promises. They promised a community charter detailing how the Council would better engage with the loyalist community etc. They eventually provided something that wasn't worth the paper it was written on.

The protest then began to take a more sinister turn. A shadowy group began attacking council property, painting the letters 292 on the doors and walls of various council buildings. Postcards were distributed through the doors of local councillors which said 'welcome to Loyalist North Down'.

The 292 painting went on for a number of weeks. It seemed to take on a life of its own, a radio show even had a physiologist on trying to work out what 292 meant. I guess that shall always remain a secret.

I got the blame of the 292 stuff but it wasn't me. Whoever it was caused some mayhem, and they seemed to do it all with nothing but a tin of paint.

It seems funny that the NIO became involved and Radio Shows were discussing it with physiologists.

I guess we will never know who was behind it unless someone decides to come forward, but I doubt they will.

The rumblings within North Down subsided for a while, and then a fresh row broke out over the Councils handling of the PEACE 3 money.

There had been some issue in Rathgill- a minor issue that could have been easily sorted- but the Council decided that instead they would refuse to release the funds to pay one of the workers their Christmas wage. I thought that was outrageous.

Along with the Rathgill Community Worker Karen Worrall I headed to North Down Borough Council and we began a sit in protest. I made the Council officer aware in no uncertain terms that we would not be leaving until we had in our hands on the cheque that would allow the worker's wages to be paid. They buckled after 4 or 5 hours and came down with the cheque. They never really did have the will for stand offs, they would always blink first and we knew that.

There were a few other protests around the PEACE 3 stuff. We ended up disrupting the Council meeting one night. We used air horns and other noisy items from the joke shop to ensure that the Council meeting could not go ahead. They were furious. The police were called and I handcuffed myself to the chair. I think the PSNI even thought the whole thing was sheer comedy. Some Councillors said they feared for their safety etc. That is the type of fantasy land they live in. A few women and local residents blow air horns and they want to be escorted to an underground bunker.

In 2011 there was another protest in North Down. That protest was really organised by another loyalist community group in the area. I took part and assisted where I could but it was their protest. The protest spent one Saturday morning blocking the main roads in and out of Bangor. Traffic was tailed back for miles and when the PSNI arrived the protestors simply moved off the road and allowed the traffic to flow again. Then they moved to another road and done the same thing. The local sergeant, who I have referred to many times in this book, was furious. He accused me of orchestrating it. I think he was really just pissed off that he was being made to look like a fool again. Maybe it was the memory of all the times he had been made look like a keystone cop that caused him to jump up and down like a little school girl when he arrested me.

I always found that it is much better to humiliate your enemies and expose them for what they are. Rioting and attacking the likes of the PSNI generates sympathy for them and your message gets lost. I have got much more success by fighting them in the courtroom. In that arena they can be exposed for what they are-and no one has any sympathy for them- but most importantly it is entirely legal to humiliate them in the courtroom and it is done by using their own rules against them.

Community work in North Down was seriously damaged by the PSNI's handling of my arrest operation. Nigel Grimshaw the Chief Superintendent shafted Tatty, a community worker who had worked on community issues with the PSNI for 16 years. They had a scheme called KEEPSAFE running; it was a drug disposal project. That was halted. Communication with the PSNI was halted and there is now a deep distrust between the community workers and the PSNI. Nigel Grimshaw was moved not long after that. Perhaps it was just rotating officers as the PSNI do, or perhaps relations with the community had become so bad that it was time for a fresh face.

Tatty Gordon was hauled before the Court for his part in my arrest. They tried to charge him with obstruction. It was crazy, absolutely crazy. Here was a community worker who had engaged with the PSNI for years, a community worker who had been asked by the senior Police officer to get me to come to his house, and then the PSNI raid that house and try and charge Tatty with obstruction. They said that Tatty called them Nazis- he didn't- that was me and I stand over the comment. That is what their behaviour reminded me of.

The court case was a farce. It cost the PSNI £1,000 to put on a security operation around the court. I have no idea why it was needed. The arresting officers all gave conflicting accounts of what happened. I think Court decorum would have me say that they had a lapse in memory or that they couldn't properly recall the incident- but this is not a Courtroom and I was never a fan of that etiquette anyway- so the truth is that I think they deliberately and maliciously lied. Lied is a big word in Court, but this is my book and in my book I am clearly stating in black and white that on numerous occasions throughout my case, Tatty's case and the cases of other flag protestors: the PSNI deliberately and maliciously contrived lies so as to try and wrongly convict people.

I haven't been overly involved in community work since my arrest. I formed a new group in Bangor called the Voluntary Education Forum; we have an office in the Towns main street. The PSNI have enquired about meeting me on a couple of occasions but I have no desire to meet them. Perhaps the individual officers are ok and genuinely want to repair relationships but sadly for them the conduct of the PSNI as a whole means that it would be impossible to build any kind of trust or relationship with the Police again. Their actions against the PUL community have been disgraceful, and I really mean that. Only recently they have arrested bandsmen for playing a musical instrument in their own community. Are they going to start arresting buskers who play musical instruments without permission from the Parades Commission?

The PSNI use ambiguous legislation and apply it when and where it suits their agenda. And let's not pretend that their agenda is not politically influenced, because it quite clearly is. There is ample evidence of that.

Ulster People's Forum

The UPF had great potential, the potential to really create a political movement that would challenge the current set up of Government. In the end we just fought on too many fronts and had too many powerful forces at work against us, but we gave it one hell of a try.

For a period we shook the political institutions. I will never forget the programme Martina Purdy done for the BBC, John Taylor praised us and Peter Robinson and Simon Hamilton ranted against us. Questions were raised about whether we could topple Peter Robinson and the power sharing executive. The Secretary of State said the flag protests constituted a National Security situation. The PSNI couldn't cope and for a couple of hours on a Friday night or at any time the protest movement had the ability to shut down the Country. The PSNI couldn't police the sheer amount of protests.

The flag protests achieved more than most people would have you believe. The protest movement had more power than we ever realised. It was only after my arrest that I realised just how much we had destabilised the political status quo. The ramifications are still being felt. The problems for power sharing started in earnest after the flag protests. We did that: you, me and every person who took to the streets in defence of the Union flag. We changed things and don't ever let anyone say we didn't.

The Ulster People's Forum had everything thrown at us. I and those around me may not have handled everything perfectly, but we did our best. The Government threw everything at shutting us down; yet we survived for over four months. In fact the protest at Belfast City Hall continues and I have nothing but the utmost respect for those people that continue the protest and keep up a presence. That takes determination.

The PSNI tried to stabilise the political situation by launching a policy of criminalising political dissent. They have done it to me for almost two years, they haven't won yet. In fact they can never win, because what can you do with a man who you couldn't buy or bully?

The UPF was the coherent voice that sought to bring together all the protestors. In essence it worked. You can't please all of the people we certainly didn't. In fact I am honest, we didn't try to. Instead we tried to do what we thought was right and take the flak from those who disagreed. If you consulted with everyone about everything then you would spend your life consulting because you would rarely get everyone agreeing.

The flag protests began on 3 December 2012 at Belfast City Hall. It was a cold night. Everyone knew the outcome. The Union flag was to be torn from the prime civic building of our capital city. The Alliance party had swung the vote in favour of Nationalists and Republicans. They say they aimed for compromise. They are fifth columnists, enemies of Unionism. They are subversives. I have dealt with the Alliance party for many years in North Down. They are opponents of Unionism and they wage their own cultural war. They want everywhere to be neutral, a cultureless culture. They are fence sitters who place themselves between the two traditions and then seek to occupy some kind of moral high ground. I don't buy that crap.

The vote went as expected, and the flag was torn down with justifiable anger erupting at City Hall. Unionists tried to break through the gates and there was chaos all over the Country. I headed back to East Belfast and was shocked to see how protestors were being treated by the PSNI. This fuelled the already palpable anger.

The chaos went on long into the night. It was only the beginning.

The following day there was talk of protests across the province, I decided to attend the protest outside Naomi Longs office on the Newtownards Road. Naomi had a hard time during the protests. She received threats and her office was attacked. There is no justification for attacks or threats against anyone but I did get rather weary of the constant victimhood portrayed by the Alliance party. Elements of the media played along with this and I got bored of it. The Alliance Party certainly played it for all it was worth. I get four or five threats every month. I live under constant threat. Yet when Naomi Long gets a threat we never hear the end of it.

The protest at the Alliance party was well attended. I was approached by a camera man who knew my face. I would have been well enough known in media circles due to community work over the years and I had already had a bit of adverse attention from the Sunday World in relation to flag disputes in the North Down area. The cameraman asked me to speak. I readily expressed my view not only on the removal of the flag but on the wider peace process. After this other cameras present approached me to speak, I was happy to do so. I saw it as an opportunity to get across my anti-agreement political viewpoint. And so it began.

The following day a protest had been organised for Newtownards. I was handed a loudhailer and asked to address the crowd. I spoke for a couple of minutes; again I spoke about wider issues and received widespread support. A video of the speech was uploaded online and it went viral across the numerous protest sites springing up.

Some so called 'loyalists' were furious about the protests erupting, I have to say I enjoyed their anger. I enjoyed seeing the peace party that many manipulated for their own financial gain coming to an abrupt halt.

After the Newtownards video I began to be contacted by organisers of other protests across the Country and invited to speak at them. It seemed that the tide had turned and finally the shift I had long predicted was taking finally taking place. The pro agreement train was grinding to a halt. This of course didn't please everyone. There were those who weren't in favour of protests, some 'loyalists' strongly expressed this view in a Radio Ulster documentary. I couldn't understand why they opposed the protests. I suspected it might be to do with their relationship with the DUP. Of course there were some elements of the loyalist community doing very well out of the 'process' but I am not going to get into all that. I have my own well known views on it. Suffice to say that those who spoke against the protests did not speak for or have any respect from me -they never will- and nor did they speak for the vast majority of the PUL community.

I began travelling around the province speaking at different rallies and protests. It seemed that most rallies attracted the same speakers. The biggest rally outside of Belfast was probably Portadown. The place was packed. The platform was me, Billy Hutchinson, Henry Reilly and Jim Allister. The microphone was broken so we had to shout. I was tired and we had been travelling to various protests all day. It turned out to be a great rally and I was proud to have attended.

We travelled some miles over those first few weeks. Rab, Roy, Jonty, wee Jim, Glenn, Michelle and Josh frequently came to various protests across the country with me.

Around this time various people began coming together to discuss how to form the protest movement into a more coherent group. And so the embryo for the Ulster Peoples Forum was created. At a meeting in South

Armagh which was attended by many of the figures within the protests and wider loyalism, it was agreed that a forum should be established to try and give a voice to the protests and to develop a long term strategy. It was decided that its initial meeting should take place in Newtownards and delegates from all over the Country would be invited.

The first meeting took place in early January and almost one hundred people turned up, representing protestors from right across the Country. It was asked that each protest send one representative to the meeting so this group of a hundred spoke for many thousands of protestors. A committee was voted in and I was chosen to be Chair of the group. I viewed it as a great honour. I still do. One particular group in North Down decided to boycott the meeting; they didn't like the anti DUP tone coming from the protests. I think I referred to them as "DUP lackeys" in a radio interview at the time. My feeling is that their real problem was that for so long certain people in North Down had portrayed themselves as speaking for the loyalist community and they had told the DUP and statutory bodies that they had control of loyalism and now it was becoming clear that it was they who were isolated as the rest of Loyalism united together.

The peace train had started to go into reverse. It was once said to me many years before the start of the protests that I should get on board the peace train or it would run over the top of me. I smiled when I saw the author of that quote flapping around trying to work out how to get things back on track for his DUP friends.

The day after the founding meeting we organised a press conference in East Belfast. Members of the media were invited and I was chairing the conference alongside other UPF committee members. It was the picture that became the mock 'McFleg' poster.

I wasn't properly dressed for the occasion. That was a mistake, it sent out the wrong message. I had been running about all day and the press conference was hastily arranged. The white winter coat made me look like something out of the East 17 boy band. The press conference was covered on every TV and radio station immediately, as well as every national newspaper the next morning.

The period after the setting up of the UPF was one of the most tiresome and stressful I have ever experienced. It was literally 24/7. We tried to organise and disseminate information the best we could but people in their eagerness demanded information instantly and continuously. That just wasn't possible. And it led to some people feeling they weren't being excluded, which is unfortunate. The problem was that we didn't have the systems or mechanisms in place to disseminate large amounts of information and hold regular meetings. I had no doubt then- and know now from my PSNI interviews in which they produced over 500 surveillance notes- that I and many around me in the UPF were under 24 hour surveillance. When discussing the protest strategy it was difficult to open the meetings too widely because the security forces were constantly placing people around us to try and destabilise things, create infighting and seeking to negatively influence the protest movement. It was hard to get a trustworthy group, but I feel we achieved that with the UPF committee.

It was also difficult because we were always very aware and conscious that the protests belonged to the people. We never wanted to be seen to try and take over the protests. It was a paradoxical situation. We decided to do our best, provide leadership for those protestors who wanted to follow us and provide support to those protestors who wanted to protest in different ways. It was all we could do. And I think it worked. There was a committed group of people- a tight knit group- the women worked tirelessly fundraising for those in prison. They deserve so much credit for what they done. They really cared about it and at great personal cost they gave themselves totally to helping their fellow protestors. I can't speak highly enough of them. They know who they are and those who matter know who they are. They are the silent, unnamed-heroes, the people that kept the protests going. If I was going to war tomorrow I would happily jump in the trenches with those women we had in the UPF.

The Forum held a strategy day in the Park Avenue Hotel in East Belfast, it was designed to create a firmer foundation for the group and try and put in place some more practical communication methods. It was well attended.

There was some disagreement over the tone of the statement to be put out by the group following the meeting. That was the first time I clashed with Willie. At the request of some protestors he had gone done to the Skainos centre. Whilst there he had spoken to Peter Robinson and this had been portrayed on the news that the UPF had engaged with the Unionist Forum. I don't think Willie should have gone near the place, though he said he genuinely didn't know what it was about and had gone to challenge Robinson. In hindsight it was a silly argument but it was indicative of the stresses and strains of the time. These things happen and it was quickly put to bed.

The Unionist Forum was the brainchild of Peter Robinson and Mike Nesbitt. I thought it was a lot of crap. It was a power grab, an attempt to stifle the protests. I know why. I wanted nothing to do with it. It was the DUP using the UUP and the others to try and create a united front that would isolate the 'extreme' protestors and give the DUP some element of control back. With this being the aim I am not surprised some supported it. I certainly didn't.

I said from the moment it was announced that I wouldn't touch it. The night before it was set to begin I was invited to Mike Nesbitt's home. He strongly expressed the view that everyone should have a stake in the Unionist Forum, to be fair to Mike I think he was genuinely trying to ensure everyone had a voice around the table. I just didn't see it that way through. There was no way I wanted to play any part in the Unionist Forum and the representatives of the Ulster Peoples Forum strongly endorsed this viewpoint. Ironically enough the Unionist forum fell flat on its face and the stand we took was vindicated.

The Ulster Peoples Forum published a comprehensive strategy document; it was an excellent piece of work. The committee developed a road show and we toured around the province holding presentations in Orange Halls, Community centres etc.

Alan Hollywood and Willie normally joined me at the front of the room. Alan would run through the presentation and me and Willie would field questions from the floor and finish with a bit of a rallying speech. Alan was very articulate, it was a shame he didn't do more media stuff during the protests. I think Alan could really be a great political representative.

The road shows went well, we got a great response and I think people really began to believe that we were getting somewhere. At the same time DUP MLAs were being chased from protests in their own areas. We had that vital ingredient to success- momentum. The only way they could halt the momentum was by effectively introducing internment by the backdoor. And that is what it was; don't be mistaken or led to believe otherwise.

The Ulster Peoples Forum began to receive invitations to meet with different groups. Two of these were the NI Policing Board and the senior command of the PSNI, at the level of ACC (Assistant Chief Constable). The committee decided we should go and Alan Hollywood, Bill Hill, Tatty Gordon and I were chosen as representatives.

Willie had been ill and off the grid for a few days. He put a tremendous amount of work into the protests and inevitably it eventually caught up with him every couple of weeks. I don't know how he managed it. I struggled with the round the clock nature of things and I am many years younger than Willie.

The meeting with the Policing Board was useful. I raised the matter of the so called weekly processions with them and asked had the PSNI given them any clarity. They said Gerry Kelly had asked the question and the Chief Constable had been unable to answer. They said it was their understanding that the PSNI were awaiting clarity around the legislation but at this stage they did not believe the walks were illegal. ACC Kerr seemed to reflect this view in his interview with Allison Morris of the Irish News.

Alan Hollywood provided an excellent visual presentation of footage he had gathered of the PSNI TSG units in action. One clip, taken from the news, showed the PSNI commander charging down the street waving his baton at anyone within his reach. He was like a man possessed. This officer was a disgrace throughout the entire period of the protests. Wherever he went there was violence. He escalated situations by inflicting needless violence on peaceful protestors.

Alan also showed the Policing Board members present footage of a horrendous attack on an elderly gentleman in East Belfast. The horrific attack was all caught on camera. Some of the board members were visibly shocked by what they saw.

By this stage relationships with the PSNI had deteriorated almost to the point of no return. I had witnessed the conduct of their TSG units, which could be compared with something you would see in North Korea. That's no exaggeration. It resulted in a palpable hatred within the loyalist community for the PSNI.

After the policing board meeting we headed to Musgrave Street PSNI station to meet with the senior PSNI command. This meeting is the subject of much debate. Two sets of minutes exist for the meeting, those taken by Pastor Mark Gordon and accepted as the truthful version of events by myself, Alan Hollywood and Bill Hill and then the notes the produced by the PSNI when they were forced to disclose information in my case. You can see Pastor Gordon's notes at the back of the book.

What is interesting is that the PPS initially said the PSNI had no record of these meetings. The interviewing officers in my case said minutes didn't exist and then they suddenly appeared and conveniently happened to suit the PSNI version of events. The PSNI minutes that appeared clearly conflicted with our minutes of the meeting. I can't help but feel this is just yet another contrived and false piece of evidence that the PSNI have put forward. That has yet to be tested in Court mind you.

The Ulster People's Forum was becoming increasingly concerned about the number of nightly arrests and the negative impact this was having within the PUL community. For this reason we decided that white line protests could be more beneficial. It would box the PSNI into a corner and leave them no option but to facilitate the protests as they were completely legal. The PSNI were told at the meeting with the UPF that this was our intention and the PSNI said they welcomed this and our commitment to keeping protests within the law.

Did I support the non-violent civil disobedience taking place such as blocking roads? Well I never condemned it. I could never publicly call for such action because to do so would have given the PSNI a free hand to arrest me for encouraging an offence. To be quite honest there were many actions taken during the flag protest that I had no problem with. I couldn't always say that publicly, but you never heard me on condemning the loyalist people. A lot of the anger was justified.

I took a lot of grief for the UPF statement calling for white line protests, but I think it was the right decision and I stand over it. Some people you could never please. Some people wanted to protest in different ways. I was always clear in saying that I personally- and the UPF as a whole- supported all protests. We suggested what way we felt was best to protest and those who chose to follow us on that well and good and those who didn't, well they still had our support.

The statement was approved by the UPF committee. Willie Frazer wasn't at the meeting: he had been unwell. I think he felt he should have been sent a copy of the statement and consulted before the decision. I felt that the majority of the committee decided that this was the way forward and so we should go with it. We issued the statement and when there was a furious reaction from Willie, I accused him of grandstanding and he accused us of trying to take control of the protests. I never really got that argument because all we were doing was speaking out for those we represented, which wasn't everyone.

I went in to pre-record an interview for the Nolan show that night. I was under real pressure that day and it felt as if I was being attacked on all sides. I remember speaking to someone very close to me and saying that I really did feel like just walking away from it all. They advised me not to;

they told me I must keep going. I am glad that for probably the one and only time I took their advice.

The situation very quickly developed into a very public row between Willie and me. I think we both said things in the media we shouldn't have said. We are both stubborn and refused to budge. It didn't do the protests any good. For a few days it became about us, and it should never have escalated to that level.

On the Saturday at the City Hall Willie approached me. There were a lot of journalists around. He said hello and I blanked him. I shouldn't have done that. Willie was my friend and it was clear he was trying to extend an olive branch. I should have accepted it. Instead I refused and thus poured petrol onto the fire which was a stupid move.

There were very few people I could trust at this stage and the pressure was intense. I did have one person I could always lean on, an unlikely person but they provided me with much needed advice. I rarely took the advice, that's a flaw in my character.

I still speak to that person pretty regularly, I trust them completely. But I still rarely take their advice- which is almost always spot on- and that pisses them off. I can understand that.

The Sunday newspapers had a field day. They called it "Union crack" and said that things between me and Willie had hit rock bottom.

I arranged a meeting with Willie in Belfast early the next week. Many newspapers had carried stories that morning talking about the end of the Ulster People's Forum. That hurt. A lot of people had invested a lot of time into building this up, and now all that work was in danger of being undone because of a petty argument between me and Willie. Our egos got in the way. I deeply regretted and at the time resolved to do everything possible to repair the situation.

We met in a bar facing the BBC. The meeting was intense, extremely heated with raised voices, finger pointing and squaring up across the table on more than one occasion. I had a close friend with me, a man who had been involved in the background of the protests from day one. He became heavily involved in the row and he and Willie went at it hammer and tongs. It is funny to look back on now but at the time it was so intense, the row could easily have turned physical. It must have been some sight for the people in having their lunch to see this playing out.

In hindsight it is exactly what was needed. It cleared the air. We shook hands and went straight to the BBC to set the record straight. The row was put behind us. It should have never got to that stage anyway. Willie and I were both as bad as each other; it was a simple lack of communication which was allowed to escalate. I hadn't helped by rudely snubbing Willie at City Hall and I later apologised to him for that.

The decision to move to white line protests suddenly began to look like a master stroke. People who initially opposed it were now warming to it and seeing the sense.

The weekly walks into Belfast City Hall continued and the UPF were asked our view on changing the route away from the Short Strand and down Middlepath Street. There were concerns that the weekly violence at the interface was damaging our cause and allowing the violent Nationalists in the Short Strand- who almost always started the trouble- to portray themselves as victims. The UPF put our name to the statement and the PSNI spoke with community representatives to confirm the arrangements. I spoke to the crowd before we left East Belfast and said that we planned to all link arms on the way home as we passed the final part of Short Strand. The idea behind this was to show the world who the violent thugs were. It wasn't my idea; it was another man who thought of it. It is a real shame that it never came to pass because I think it would have been an amazing sight.

On the way back from City Hall it became apparent that the PSNI had pulled a move. They had blocked the bridge and left only one road open, the road that led directly past the Markets and towards the Short Strand. It was a trap, they wanted the protestors to follow that path so as they could then present us as rampaging thugs. I along with others spoke with the police at the bridge but by this stage it was too late, thousands of people had headed down the only street left open and towards the Short Strand. I can understand why the protestors went down the only road available to us. The PSNI had reneged on an agreement and proved yet again that they could not be trusted.

Violent Republicans emerged from the Short Strand and began to attack the peaceful protestors returning home. Thugs wearing masks and throwing bottles, bricks and much more appeared from the Short Strand. They had prepared in advance to launch their attack. They held a banner with my name threatening to kill me; the PSNI went in to remove the banner in the midst of the riot. The Republican thugs spotted me and began directing many of their missiles in my direction. This was only a couple of nights after I had been hit by a brick live on television at Pitt Park (Lower Newtownards

Road). What is more concerning however is that people who live on these interface areas are constantly being attacked. I don't live there; I don't have to suffer the nightly attacks. What is the Government doing for the people who have their homes and property attacked on a daily basis? Where are the benefits of the so called peace process for these people?

The PSNI and Sinn Fein reaction to the Saturday mayhem was comical. Gerry Adams said no one in the Short Strand had been firing missiles or throwing anything. Matt Baggott apologised to the people of the Short Strand-Bizarre.

The Sunday papers all carried the coverage of the Saturday riot. They tried to put the blame onto the protestors- exactly what the PSNI wanted. I rejected that outright and was strong in my view that the PSNI had set a trap for the protestors. The Sunday Life carried a picture of me and Winkie Irvine of the PUP behind PSNI lines talking with the officer in charge. We were trying to get them to pull back so as to allow Protestors who had been trapped in the middle to get back through. (The PSNI had initially tried to charge me for obstruction for this, even though it was they who asked us to come through and speak to the senior officer. They soon backtracked on that one once that was put to them).

On the Wednesday night I was invited onto the BBC1 Nolan show. Jim Wilson from East Belfast was also present. As I came into the studio a round of applause broke out. The place with packed with loyalists. Chris Donnelly, a republican commentator- who is as bitter as they come- tweeted furiously that there were too many loyalists in the place due to the applause I received when I came in to the building. Sinn Fein later made a formal complaint to the BBC.

That Nolan Show attracted one of the biggest audiences of the year. It has been watched online thousands of times. I publicly challenged Gerry Kelly saying that he had a cheek criticising me when I wasn't the one who shot a prison officer in the head. That sentence was remembered above everything else I said. Jim Wilson put photos on the table showing the violent republicans from the Short Strand attacking peaceful protestors. For 15 minutes solid on the show it bounced from me to Jim and back again as we relentlessly tore into Sinn Fein and the Alliance party. Gerry Kelly didn't like it. He wasn't used to it. It was great TV and it got a massive reaction.

The week after the bridge debacle it was agreed that the various protest groups would together issue a statement to call for the walk to pass down Middle path Street to avoid the potential for violence emanating from the

Short Strand. This was a hard sell but the protestors embraced the idea. The PSNI eventually tried to charge me for taking part in this, even though they facilitated and encouraged this route.

If indeed they contend I am guilty then ACC Kerr, Mark McEwan and Alan McCrum are equally guilty yet I don't see them on trial. Of course not, that would be politically inconvenient. They needed a political scapegoat to pin their failings on and they tried to make me that scapegoat. What they didn't factor in was that I would fight them tooth and nail the whole way. They expected me to make some kind of plea bargain and they could bury it all. They soon realised they had made a serious error of judgement.

The Friday night protests also continued. Operation Standstill was the name given to these protests. They shut the Country down for a couple of hours when traffic couldn't move.

The PSNI and the Government couldn't understand the flag protests. It was something they had never experienced before. Social media played a big role. It was unpredictable, the direction was constantly changing and there was no way for them to stop it. Every person played an equal role and had an equal stake in the protest. They couldn't understand that, it was something different.

So they lashed out, the needed scapegoats and people like me ended up bearing the brunt of their political persecution. But many other protestors suffered greatly, many suffered much more than I did. There were hundreds of cases of human rights violations and there is a lot of archived footage of PSNI TSG units wading into peaceful protestors with batons. They beat women, children and pensioners. Some of the PSNI officers were full of bloodlust in my opinion. They couldn't wait to inflict violence onto protestors.

People reading this may think that never happened. Our police force is too civilised, too professional for that to happen. Watch the footage for yourself and ask other people who became the victim of their political persecution. They will tell you about the real PSNI.

I ended up in jail and have then been under the jackboot of PSNI bail conditions for almost two years. Do I regret my role in the flag protests? Not for a minute. We achieved something that had never been done in this Country before. We brought forward a kind of protest driven by social media and the power of ordinary people that was never seen before in the UK, and is unlikely to be seen again. It was a National Security situation to use the words of the Secretary of State. It shook the sham of a peace process to its very core and the ramifications are still being felt. Things will never be the same after the flag protests. It forced the appeasement process to a halt.

The Orange Order said this generation owed the flag protestors a great deal. They said we awoke a generation from their slumber and that they were sleepwalking into a United Ireland. If the flag protests achieved nothing else, then that was good enough for me.

The Men Who Don't Exist

I received a telephone call from a trusted friend and they said that someone wanted to meet with me. I was told the meeting had to be strictly confidential but the person had some information that they wanted to pass on to me.

I met with my friend and this individual who I will refer to as X. When I realised just who the individual was, I understood the magnitude of the information I was about to be provided with.

The man told me that the information I was about to be given would breach the Official Secrets Act. He said he would tell me some particular questions to ask and these questions would lead to the truth.

I questioned X about why he wanted to give the information to me. He said he was fed up with the cover up's and the lies. He had devoted his life to fighting the IRA and now the very same people were controlling policing and justice. I completely understood his motivation.

I was shown some documents and told to take notes. The documents proved to me what X was telling me were true. It was scary stuff. He told me the COBRA committee had been briefed about this and that the Government and the Secretary of State knew.

X assisted me in formulating a list of questions. The questions are in the book section called 'OTR Scheme- the questions that must be answered'.

I would never betray the confidence of the man who came and give me that information. I have no doubt that he saw me as a little more than a good conduit to get his information into the public. But I didn't mind that: let's be honest, it suited my political agenda.

I immediately formulated the information I had been provided into a list of questions. Some were red herrings, he told me that, but he assured me that if I could find a way of getting the questions asked then it would reveal the truth. He told me that Royal Pardons had been given to senior members of the IRA. This was not public knowledge. I raised the issue on social media and was laughed at and called a fantasist, a conspiracy theorist.

I wrote the questions up and sent them to Kate Hoey MP. I trusted Kate and I knew she would genuinely seek answers. Kate raised a question with the Secretary of State. The answer was startling. The Secretary of State admitted that indeed Royal Pardons had been issued, but conveniently they had lost many of the details. Newtown Emerson of the Irish News wrote a column the next day and remarked that it was a remarkable story that an MP had asked some of the questions that had been included in my document and indeed it had exposed that what I had been saying was not fantasy, it was true.

It seems bad enough that some of these IRA terrorists received pardons but the real truth behind many of the Royal Pardons is much more frightening. Many of those who received these pardons were working as paid State agents. They were being run by MI5. In essence these men who had committed horrific atrocities had done so whilst being paid British assets. MI5 had allowed these people to carry out brutal attacks on ordinary British citizens, British Soldier's and members of the RUC and UDR. They did so under the cloak of National Security. They then pressed the Government to issue Royal Pardons to ensure that their assets would never face a court trial and therefore MI5's involvement would remain hidden under a cloak of secrecy.

A few days after this I met with X again and on this occasion he was able to give me copies of some documents. I took the photocopies of the documents away and he warned me that MI5 would not want this being exposed. I contacted a member of the NI Select Affairs committee at Westminster and shared the information I had received. I said it was now quite obvious that many of those in receipt of OTR letters and Royal Pardons were being handled by MI5. The response was a simple one: *"yes, we think so to."*

I was leaving the back of my house and walking up the entry when two men came towards me. I thought nothing of it as they did not look in any way threatening. I went to pass the two men when suddenly the dark haired man on my right hand side put his arm out to stop me. I said *"what the fuck are you doing."* He replied *"no need to be aggressive Jamie, we just want to talk"* I stared back at him waiting for him to say something else but it was the other man who spoke this time, he said: *"Jamie, we are the people that are responsible for ensuring that the scales of society are* balanced but if someone starts trying to tip those scales then that upsets the balance of things. And society needs balance Jamie, do you understand?" I said that I was quickly coming to understand who they were. They then said *"we are not here to cause you problems Jamie, we are just letting you know that past history proves that those unbalancing the scales usually not stay around for long"* I became agitated *"Who the fuck do you think you are talking to you prick, I want to see your badges, what station are you from? Who are you? I will be reporting this to the local PSNI"* Both men then stood aside and calmly replied *"good luck with that, we are the men who don't exist. We'll see you soon."* They walked on down the entry and I immediately phoned my solicitor. They got into a dark blue car and I took down the registration. I informed my solicitor of the encounter and he advised me to go and report it to the PSNI.

I went down to the station and spoke to the local commander. He was a decent enough man, ex RUC. He smiled when I told him what had happened and simply said *"I am not surprised."* The PSNI said they knew nothing about it and I believed them. My solicitor said it was more than likely MI5 or some other shady branch of British Intelligence.

That occasion was the first time I had been openly approached. Weeks later I was out for a social night with my good friend Gary Halliday. His wife was away for the week so we decided to head into the town on a Friday night, just the two of us. We went to a local bar and had a few drinks. Within half an hour a female attempted to join our company, she was being extremely flirty and hands on with me. I knew straight away what was going on and alerted Gary. He watched for a couple of minutes then decided to confront her. When he asked if she was undercover, suddenly the women who had previously appeared extremely drunk, was as sober as a judge. She ignored Gary and looked at me as she threw a few names of well known Loyalists my direction saying they were friends of hers. That would have been plausible if not for the fact they had mostly been dead for 10 years or more so there was no way of verifying her story. I suppose it was a good attempt at a cover story. I told her that just like Gary I knew exactly what she was up to. With this she purposely knocked a drink over from the table and pretending to be extremely drunk left the bar. One of the doormen watched her as she staggered for 100 yards and then started walking normally and got into a silver car. We decided to leave this bar and Gary said he needed to go to the bank machine. I would always be pretty security conscious and I noticed a suspicious car with tinted windows at the bottom of the street. Out of the corner of my eye I saw a fair haired man get out of the back of the car. As Gary went to the bank I sat on a small ledge and the man I had just witnessed getting out of the car started staggering up the street, he then made a beeline towards me and pretending to look surprised he said *"Jamie Bryson, amazing to meet you"* He was Welsh. I said cheers mate and walked towards Gary, he grabbed my arm saying *"it is wrong what is happening to you, it very wrong but not everyone is like the PSNI"* I clicked straight away what he was at. I made my excuses and headed over to Betty Blacks, a local bar/club. Gary and I continued drinking and having a good time. Suddenly up beside us popped this fair haired man. He pretended not to see us, and then ever so obviously bumped into Gary. I decided to humour him. I asked him where he was from *"Wales mate, I am a diver and I am just in the area for the weekend"* I near burst out laughing. What a poor cover story. I asked him if he was alone and he said that he was the only one of his team staying in Bangor. Unprompted he then produced a driving licence, the only problem was it was Northern Ireland driving licence with an address in Portrush. Gary has low tolerance of these people so in no uncertain terms he highlighted to him that he was full of shit and moreover, he was a pretty poor intelligence gatherer.

The man ignored Gary's comments. I always find it startling how they just pretend they didn't hear when they have been rumbled and continue on. As if we will just forget.

He then decided to say he was in an Orange Lodge in Wales. I got bored and when I said *"would you ever fuck off and tell your bosses to stop sending arseholes like you into my company. It won't work"* he clearly knew his cover was blown and glanced over his shoulder. Betty Blacks has mirrors behind the bar. As I looked in the mirror I saw two heavy gentlemen sitting at a directly table behind me, drinking Fanta Orange. I hadn't noticed them. Knowing he was rumbled our Welsh friend went for the jugular *"Jamie, some people are supportive of you, people who aren't the PSNI, if you get me. There are people that could make you very powerful, it just has to be done the right way"* I laughed in his face. He smiled, shrugged his shoulders and headed for the door. The two heavies behind me got up thirty seconds later and one of them tapped Gary saying *"I think I recognise you, well I definitely know your face"* he then turned and walked out the door.

A couple of minutes later a friend of mine who was on the door came into the bar looking for me. He was unaware of what had happened but he said he had come to warn me that the fella who he had spotted sliding up beside me at the bar had just left and been picked up by a waiting car. He thought it looked dodgy. He was right.

I have been under constant surveillance for the past two years. When I was interviewed by police they had over 500 logs over a three month period. You can listen to my PSNI interview tapes and hear this for yourself. They had been able to tell me my movements, who I met and where I went from times when I would have no idea I was being followed. The cost of this must be astronomical. It is shocking given the fact that I am merely a political activist; I am not plotting terrorism or violence.

I raised this matter with a local PSNI officer during a conversation outside my office one day. What he said was interesting *"Jamie, the PSNI investigate crime. That is what we are responsible for. Of course we are briefed to occasionally stop you search you and the usual stuff but all the pressure you are getting isn't coming from us. As I said, we investigate crime and you aren't a criminal. You would be viewed as a political threat, a threat to the stability of the peace process and that puts you under the remit of MI5. Look in that direction. We only occasionally provide logistical support."* It was pretty much an admission. He was telling me that MI5 were watching me and the PSNI only occasionally provided logistical support. I assume by logistical support he meant surveillance but I can't be sure. It would have been great to have been able to take that conversation to the Police Ombudsman but to do so I would have had to name the officer, and I wouldn't have done that. He was ex RUC and I felt he was telling me something in good faith. I also knew that his political views weren't a million miles from mine. I wouldn't have sunk him.

It was a cold night as I came to my house. I had made a copy of some of the documents I had been given by X and placed them in a brown folder. They were secured in my house. I usually keep nothing in the house but I had decided to take the chance for a couple of hours. I was going to South Londonderry the following day to meet a friend and pass copies of the documents onto him. We had worked together on political stuff for a number of years. A lot had been done in the background to expose elements of the Claudy bomb. (An account of that particular atrocity as told by a security forces source can be found in Part Two of this book.)

I brought the brown folder out and placed it in the back seat of my car. You can see it clearly in the photographs section of the book. I locked my car and went into the house for the night.

I was up early the next morning, had some breakfast and was just opening the door when I saw a van arrive with cameras on top of it. They looked as if they were clamping my car. I got my shoes on and ran out of the house. *"What do you think you are doing with my car?"* he had already clamped it. I lost my temper and started moving towards him *"You are on camera Jamie, you are on camera"* he began shouting as he kept retreating. It came into my head that this was a trap; if I said or did anything I would be immediately arrested. I stopped in my tracks and stared at him. He was clinging to the door of his van like a rabbit caught in the headlights. You coward I thought to myself.

They drove of and I lifted the notice left on my windscreen, unpaid parking tickets. I couldn't believe it. What a nonsense I thought. I had an appointment in Bangor so I got a lift over and decided I would ring up and sort the car when I got back. As I was leaving Donaghadee my anger got the better of me. I rang the DRD and told them I was deeply unhappy with the situation and explained my objections to the parking fines. I cannot go into this in too much detail as it is currently the subject of an internal DRD investigation and judicial proceedings. The long and short of it is that the DRD representative had assured me the car would not be lifted until the issues I had raised were resolved. Fair enough I thought.

When I returned home my car had been lifted, despite the assurances that it would not be. I spoke to a neighbour who told me they couldn't believe the amount of people who had come to lift the car. They came with an army because they were quite obviously cowards.

The issue with the DRD was resolved the next morning. I had a number of robust conversations with the Minister Danny Kennedy. To be fair he was very helpful and promptly addressed the issues I had raised.

I went to the pound in Templepatrick to collect my car. When I arrived the pound manager informed me that the PSNI had been out and searched my car earlier in the day. I exploded. I angrily shouted at the pound manager and his assistant. I felt bad about this. The poor lady assistant had only been doing her job; I took my anger out on the wrong person. I deeply regretted that and later apologised for my reaction.

The pound manager handed me a piece of paper with the name of an officer, his mobile number and his extension number. I rang the mobile and he answered, I began by saying *"Alright there, its Jamie Bryson here, I believe you were snooping around my car today like a little rat"* there was silence and then he said *"how did you get this number"* I laughed and replied *"you are not exactly James Bond are you, you left it on a piece of paper at the pound. But never mind that, where is the search warrant? Where is the sheet of paper detailing what was taken?"* he hung up. I rang back and said *"Who do you think you are hanging up, if you are going to illegally snoop around my car I want the correct paperwork"* he said he would arrest me for harassment if I rang again. He was from the serious organised crime branch, some task force set up to investigate loyalism.

I rang my solicitor and he immediately contacted the PSNI and came back to me saying that he had been promised the warrant would be faxed straight away. The officer had claimed their printer was broken and that is why they didn't have any warrant to leave at the pound. That is a lie. There never was a warrant.

I went down with the pound manager and looked at my car. The brown folder was gone. Nothing else was touched. The boot wasn't even opened, I know this because my sports bag was there piled high and it hadn't moved. I knew there was something very wrong with this whole situation. I rang my solicitor back and explained the situation. We agreed we needed to get the CCTV from the pound to see the search, which was carried out without a warrant, and catch them red handed. I told the pound manager I would need the CCTV. He made a call and came back out and said this wouldn't be a problem.

I went to the Ombudsman the next day and put forward my complaint. I especially wanted to know how the PSNI knew my car was there, why a warrant had not been produced and why they had taken the brown folder from the car.

A few weeks later the Ombudsman came back to me with disturbing news. The CCTV from the day in question wasn't available. It had apparently been broken on that day. What a co-incidence eh? The warrant still hadn't been forthcoming either, I wonder why? The officer told both me and my solicitor that he would send us it.

A few weeks went by and the Ombudsman came back to me. There was no warrant. The PSNI were now saying that because the car had been seized by the DRD, the DRD were the legal owners of the car for that period of 24 hours and due to the fact they had let the PSNI search the car there was no need for a warrant. It was a legal grey area and the PSNI had once again used their power to exploit it. The officer who searched the car was a liar. He lied to me and he lied to my solicitor and then he got together with others and contrived to bend the law in order to cover them. It is more often than not the PSNI who are the criminals.

ACC Drew Harris was pulled by a prominent Westminster politician about it, he was lost for words.

The Ombudsman report came back and found that there was insufficient evidence to substantiate my complaint. Of course there was.

The CCTV had magically vanished, they had got the car into the DRD pound which they then claimed made the DRD legal owners (this will be tested in Court via a judicial review) and because they gave the PSNI permission to search my car. They just happened to be aware that the car was there and just out of interest they decided to casually head up for a wee look in the hope that it would be unlocked. The car was locked. I know that for a fact. They say it just happened to be open.

It is all just one big co-incidence. They accept the file vanished and they accept that it was in my car when my car was lifted. But they can't explain why it wasn't there when I came to collect it (DRD photographs prove that it wasn't there when I came to lift the car but was there when they put it on the lorry to take it to the pound) but they say they didn't take it and guess what- the CCTV that would prove them as liars has disappeared.

That is how the PSNI operate. Perhaps this was one of the occasions where they were providing 'logistical support' to MI5. I would bet my life it was!

It is just as well the brown folder contained only copies of the information, information that is already with some MP's.

I met X not long after this and he warned me to be careful. MI5 were apparently furious that the Royal Pardons had come to light and he felt that they would do everything and anything to ensure that the revelations stopped there. I didn't doubt him for one minute.

It sounds like a fantasy land, but it is not. It is what is really going on but until you experience it your mind can't accept the gravity of it. We are conditioned to think that our Government and the Security Forces are transparent, that they are good people who would never do anything wrong. We are conditioned to believe that the Government wouldn't have their own people killed to ensure that the 'balance' is maintained. But they would.

The Queen herself has said that there are forces at work within the UK that even she has no control over. I was recently handed another document by a former member of the RAF. It contained information about the

Chinook helicopter crash just before the ceasefires. It has been said that many of those on the flight co-incidentally-or not so co-incidentally- opposed making peace with the IRA. That file contains flight logs that conflict the official account given amongst other extremely sensitive material.

The file is now in the hands of people who will be able to piece together the events of that day much better than I. One thing is for sure, the truth is vastly different than what the British people have been led to believe.

A few years prior to the protests I had been working alongside another man trying to expose the cover up around the Claudy bomb because so many questions about that atrocity remain unanswered. I was given a recording of Ivan Cooper explaining what he said happened. An IRA man had come to him and confessed his role in the bombing. There is an article that was given to me a few years ago called 'Who Judges the Judges'. I have included it in the second part of this book. It goes into more detail about what allegedly happened during the cover up of the bombing. What I do know for a fact is that the PSNI have evidence that proves the PIRA carried out the bombings. That particular forensic evidence shows the same bomb maker that made two other bombs that were claimed by the IRA also made the Claudy bomb. He was known as 'Bomber blew' and he was from Bellaghy in Co. Londonderry.

The PSNI and the security services hide behind National Security to cover many of their dirty deeds. The truth is that many of these deeds are not done for the greater good or to protect us, they are done to protect the political elite and ensure the right people stay in power and thus the right 'balance' is maintained.

I was approached not long ago by a friend. A contact of his had approached him and told him to warn me that a local business had been bugged by the PSNI and that they were seeking to gather evidence by eavesdropping on my conversations. I wasn't shocked by this. I have been aware for some time that the PSNI are using such techniques. I regularly take great pleasure in going off on a tangent if I suspect I am being listened to, feeding them full of fantasy. It's no more than they deserve.

A number of my friends and associates have also been approached and offered money or other incentives to provide information on me. What information is it they want? I know that they want to know who X is because I was approached by an off duty PSNI officer not long ago. He randomly struck up a conversation in a shopping centre and began asking how my case was going. He then ever so gently steered the conversation around to trying to draw it out of me where I was getting the OTR information and what he described as COBRA documents. They must think I am daft.

The Haass talks were billed as the big compromise, the talks that would sort everything out. I opposed them from the beginning. The PUL community have nothing left to give, so what is the logical reason to enter talks that aim to find a compromise? We have nothing left to compromise on.

I went up to the talks in the final days. People from the UUP and DUP had been in touch via the phone, they wanted to hear my views on the proposals.

The draft Haass documents were meant to be secret, only those in the room were allowed to view them and they weren't allowed to leave the building. So I was asked to come to the building.

I don't think it was policy from the UUP or DUP to show me or Willie Frazer the documents. It was individuals within those groups who were reasonably sympathetic to our more hard line views.

I went into the toilets and was passed a shorthand copy of the documents. I was given 15 minutes to study the document whilst the person who had given me it went to make a phone call. He returned after 15 minutes and took back the paperwork he had given me. I expressed my disgust at what I had read and he promised to keep me up to date. He said he would deny this exchange ever took place, I said that he didn't have to worry; I would never reveal my source.

On the final night I was at the Stormont hotel in early evening, I was receiving occasional text updates. In the middle of the evening I received a call from a senior Ulster Unionist. He told me that Nesbitt had tried to sell the deal to the party executive but that it had been dismissed outright. He told me that the continuation of the talks later into the night were pointless because Mike Nesbitt couldn't sell it to the party executive and therefore the UUP wouldn't be signing up to any deal. Another person in my company received a text message saying something similar.

About half an hour after this I again met my original source at the far end of the car park, well out of sight. He told me the DUP didn't think there would be a deal anyway, but now that the UUP weren't going to agree, they too (the DUP) would be dismissing the proposals. I was told the continuation of talks were fruitless, it would end in failure.

I went on home and tweeted that there wouldn't be a deal. There was confusion as to how I knew this information and who had given it to me. The talks were still ongoing.

The row over how Willie Frazer and I knew so much information and whether we were being briefed by the Unionist parties rumbled on for a couple of days. The UUP and DUP denied that there was any corporate party decision to brief us. That was the truth. Those who were talking to me were doing so off their own bat. I don't know who was talking to Willie.

There is many within the UUP and DUP that would regularly speak to me. Sometimes they will leak me information about their party that they know I will use. Most times this is part of internal party politics, but it suits my agenda to expose what is going on. There was one such recent incident after Edwin Poots, Paul Givin and Paul Frew were sacked from their posts. The official DUP line was that there was a reshuffle.

The day after Poots had been sacked I was contacted by a reliable source within the DUP, someone who is perceived to be close to Peter Robinson but who in reality is working to have him removed. They told me that a DUP executive meeting had taken place the day prior to Edwin Poots being sacked. I was told that Poots challenged Robinson on the deal he had with the SOS to re-engage in a talk's process. In return for this the SOS agreed to implement some kind of whitewashed panel of inquiry into the North Belfast parading situation. The 'source' also said that Edwin Poots had been saying at the meeting that the DUP should not be entering any talks because the Unionist community had nothing left to give. Robinson was incensed. Paul Frew and Paul Givin spoke in support of Edwin Poots. All three were sacked the next day.

I released a press statement detailing the information I had been given. The Newsletter ran it as their front page the next day. Sam McBride did his best to have a dig at me in the article. I am not sure why, he had just run a front page story and accepted that no one, including the media, had the faintest idea about what had really gone on inside the DUP until I broke the story.

I am not a fan of Sam McBride anyway. I think he has an agenda and he comes across as very arrogant.

Past, Present and Future

I decided to give up playing football just before the start of the current season (14/15). I just wasn't enjoying it anymore. There was no excitement on a Saturday; it was more like a chore.

I decided that I would give management a shot as I figured that I would be pretty good at it. One of my qualities is as a leader, I have the ability to make decisions and stand over them and aside from that I have played at a high enough level myself before I lost interest. I played at Linfield, Crusaders and Bangor. I played a few games for Bangor's first team against Glentoran, Lisburn Distillery and Donegal Celtic. I represented my County at the Milk Cup. I had trials at Manchester United and from I was 14 I played men's football in the afternoons.

I played my youth football for St Andrews FC. We had a fantastic team and a wonderful manager. Stefan Seaton was like a father figure to all the boys in the team, he taught me everything I know about football and his methods have certainly influenced how I now coach my own team. There is a difference between fear and respect, I wouldn't say I have ever really feared anybody, but there was an unbelievable respect there for Stefan and there still is. Even now I would ring him up for a chat or to ask his advice.

He has almost won the Milk Cup with his Co. Antrim team on a couple of occasions- that is a big thing. County teams just don't get to finals or win Milk Cups, but somehow Stefan manages to make young lads farfetched dreams become reality year after year.

I got injured playing for Linfield youth team and missed half a season. The youth team was managed by Jim Thompson and his son Johnny, they are very well respected people within football and I have a lot of time for them. I had some great craic during the season I spent playing for their team.

I went on to Crusaders and played a season in the reserve team there before picking up an injury in a game at Seaview, against Linfield ironically.

Jeff Spiers was my reserve team manager at Crusaders: I liked him and his assistant Paul Foy. Paul had that much ability he could probably still play at a decent level and he must be touching 50.

I went to Bangor after that and played in the first team for Paul Miller all through pre-season. I got injured again and pretty much lost interest after that. I floated about the amateur league for a couple of years but I had no interest. I ended up playing for Groomsport because I had a long time affiliation with the club.

I would still say that deep down Groomsport are my club. I was around it from it was 7 or 8 years of age and I made some fantastic friends there over the years- people like Owen, John, Ian and Billy.

Owen managed one of the Groomsport senior teams when I was 14 or so, he asked me to come and play for him a few times to help out, I was happy to. I was always a difficult player for managers; after I left Stefan I didn't have the best attitude in the world but I never fell out with Owen. If he rang me up today and asked me to go anywhere and play for him, I would be there in an instant.

When I had went to Groomsport after I had lost interest Ian Patton was the manager. I have known Ian from childhood; I always was very friendly with him. He tried hard as manager of the team, assisted by Gary during a difficult period for the club. I wasn't very helpful and my attitude wasn't great. I regret that deeply and I regret the hassle that my attitude caused for Ian and people at the club who really are my friends. I was pre-occupied with loyalist activities and football was little more than a distraction.

1st Bangor is a great club with a great set up and they offered me the job of managing their Second team. It is all young lads that just lack a bit of discipline and direction. I was more than happy to take up the offer. I had taken on the role for 9 games at the tail end of last season (13/14) and turned it around for them, they went 9 games unbeaten with some great wins. Above all else I thought it would give me a different kind of challenge.

The first team managers are Gary McKibben and Mark Knell. I have known Gary for 15 years as his son Graeme was St Andrews goalkeeper right through our youth football. Graeme is now 1st choice keeper with Ards FC and is still a friend of mine. I laughed a couple of seasons ago when he got a bet up, went and spent it all on a big flash jeep and then realised he could hardly afford to put petrol in it, typical.

My team is full of fellas aged from 16 to 21. They are a really decent group of lads and I enjoy working with them.

Brett Hamilton was a winger when I got him, which was never his position. I made him into a defensive mid-field player or a sweeper and I honestly believe that Brett has the potential to play football in the Irish League. He has the attitude and he has the ability, he is far too good for the team he is in.

There are other lads with potential as well. Rory plays up front but he is lazy. Ability hangs out of him but he doesn't have the work rate off the ball. We are working on that.

Robbie Irvine is like a chubby Paul Gascoigne, I think he could play at the top level of the Amateur league. I have a smashing Goalkeeper as well in David Middleton, he is only 18. He is a loyalist originally from Scotland and that endears him to me that wee bit more.

All the lads are really good people with plenty of character. Big Kurtis Kane is like a child, it is genuinely like babysitting when he is in your company. He does security for me if I am going to Court in Belfast or somewhere that has the potential to be a bit dodgy. On one occasion I asked where he was after he had come to Court with me, the other fella looked on in disbelief as he told me that Kurtis had decided to go for a McDonalds because he was hungry. He said that Kurtis had added that he thought any trouble makers would likely be at McDonalds anyway. He was deadly serious.

My captain is a lad called Luke Kelly; I went to school with him. He is a really decent guy and very loyal, I like that in a person. He has really become more like a friend since I got involved in the football team.

I am assisted by David Nannery. He has been a friend of mine for the guts of ten years. He is in his late 40's but he can party with the best of them. He shouts and screams until he almost blows the house down, but he means well. I like him, if I didn't I wouldn't have him about me. I had a few hilarious experiences out and about with Davy, I was almost tempted to put them in the book but I couldn't quite bring myself to. What goes on tour...

I hope to continue in football management, it is a challenge and I have got the buzz back. It gives me another interest in life which is important.

I am not so sure that I have a future as an elected political representative; I don't think I have the patience or a high enough tolerance for lies. I intended to stand in the local Government and European Elections this year but I had to withdraw late on. The truth is that I found out my partner was due to have a child. The elections would have placed a lot of stress on her and that is why I announced that I would be taking a step back from politics. I resolved to stay in the shadows. It lasted a while but if truth be told I missed the hustle and bustle of it, I missed living on the edge and I missed the natural thrill.

Some people are addicted to smoking, some to drinking and some to drugs; I think my addiction is the buzz you get from living in the danger zone. I think you get used to the adrenaline and when it's not there you start to crave it. That maybe sounds a bit strange, but it's the truth of how I feel. Maybe my body and mind have just adapted to living in a constant state of high alert and when I am not in that place I miss the adrenaline rush. I can't explain it any other way.

I sometimes wish that I could just live the quiet life, working 9-5 and going out with friends and family at the weekends, but then again that wouldn't really fulfil me. I don't think I would be happy. I think I would be miserable.

My personality thrives in conflict and fighting against the odds, I don't enjoy tranquillity. I have always been like that, maybe that will change in later life but who knows.

Even when I go on holiday I can't relax, after a few days I can't wait to get back to the hustle and bustle of life in N.Ireland.

I went on holiday to Turkey in July of this year. I had a really good time, but even then I spent the majority of my time in the Rangers bar. I met Curtis and Abbie, a really lovely young couple from Scotland. We have since become good friends. Big Ian Rae and his family also became friends of ours on that holiday; I hope to catch up with them again soon.

I always think it is really important to remember and stay loyal to your real friends in life. It is very easy sometimes to forget your real friends. I try not to do that. I have friends like Gary Halliday who I know I can always count on. Then there is Tatty, he has never once let me down.

I also have people like Jay and Rab who are two friends that I have a real bond with. You can't manufacture that kind of trust that comes from loyalty, the kind of trust that if I was in the trench's tomorrow I would want those two friends with me and I think they would probably want me with them as well. Many have tried to whisper behind backs and maliciously contrive to break the bond between us, but those kinds of people cannot understand real friendship or how it is forged.

They cannot grasp that there are some people who would never turn on their friends; there are some people who would sacrifice themselves before they would shaft their own. I know this because there have been times when those two friends stood by me and didn't even tell me about it;

because that is just what you do for your friends. I am privileged to have them around me and to be around them.

I try to stay in touch with my friends from school as well. I enjoyed school. I had a PE teacher called Stuart Donald, what a great guy. I still keep in touch with him. The education system needs teachers like Stuart Donald. They don't just teach the curriculum, they teach you life lessons.

As I mentioned during the introduction David Gibson and William Newberry were my best friends from school. I would do anything for them. William has recently moved away to England to start a new life with his partner, I was really sorry to see him go but we will keep in touch. I hope he can still make our yearly trips to Old Trafford. I will never forget that European Cup Final in Moscow. *"Believe wee man"*.

I recently found out that like me, David is to be a father next year. It is hard to believe. I remember meeting David in the first day of high school like it was yesterday. He supported Wolves, I couldn't believe that. I still can't. His family are good people as well.

I made many good friends over the last few years, people like wee Davy and Sammy. They are true loyalists and I don't give that description lightly.

I also became friends with Bobby Matthesion when I started going to Bangor Elim Church. He is a former UVF life sentence prisoner who has now devoted his life to working as a Christian to help people. His whole family are wonderful people and have been very supportive of me. There is so much potential in the work that Bobby does and I really hope that all his hard work and effort bears fruit for Gods Kingdom. Keep a watchful eye out for his young sons as well, two great footballers who genuinely have the potential to become stars.

Mark, Tina, Ally and Louie Ferguson are also close family friends. I value their friendship.

As I said at the very start of this book, I hope for a future where N.Ireland is a peaceful and tranquil place, that isn't for my benefit, it is for the benefit of my children and future generations. In N.Ireland we live in a divided society of us and them. That doesn't really bother me, although I can't help but think that things could be so much better for us all.

The previous generations that currently hold the political power in this Country cannot bring us to a better place, that is the job of my generation and those that come behind us. When the time comes to build a real and genuine peace, there will be no place at the table for the likes of me.

The real peace can never come while we continue to implement the current process of appeasement that will see the PUL community become second class citizens and the Country we hold so dear robbed off us.

To get to the point where real peace can be built, the false peace must be resisted at all costs.

David McCann the political commentator asked me during an interview how I would like to be remembered. I had never really thought about it then, but I have now.

Some people will remember me as someone who was in the limelight, who was all about himself, but those people don't know me and their viewpoint is most likely coloured by jealously, outright hatred or their own political agenda.

I *hope* those who do know me will remember me as someone who devoted his life to the cause of Ulster, our people and the freedom of our future generations.

I *hope* my friends remember me as someone who was loyal to a fault, as someone who always stood by his own and as someone who would stand by his friends no matter what the personal cost.

I *hope* my children look up to me and realise that I took the stand I did because in my heart I genuinely believed it was right. I hope that I will be a good father, a good step father and a good husband.

I *hope* my Mum, Dad, Nana and Grandfather never has to remember me, I hope I will always be here for the duration of their lives. They are special people.

Those are the ways in which I *hope* to be remembered.

"Ah hope, the last temptation" said Dietrich Bonheoffer as he was offered to renounce his beliefs, join the Nazis and in return be allowed to live. He was hung before he would betray everything he stood for.

Money will never buy me and threats will never silence me. The only way to deal with a man like me is to put a bullet in the back of my head. I am sure many would love to and if that is what is to be- then that is what is to be- it is God's will.

I will continue to do what I feel is right for the Protestant people of this Country and what is right for our future generations. I won't be lying awake worrying about the consequences of that. *"Watch the wind and trust the Lord"*.

Long Live Loyal Ulster!

PART 2

This part of the book contains a number of articles and documents that I have written relating to Loyalism, the peace process and the political institutions. Some of the articles have not previously been in the public domain.

*The 'Implications of the Haass process' document was published by the Ulster Human Rights Watch.

The Equality Agenda- National identity diluted!

Equality is one of the new buzz words within the peace process. When twisted in the correct manner it conjures up the necessary moral high ground and therefore is an effective tool when seeking to use it to achieve otherwise political ends and the destruction of a particular National identity or expression of civic/community culture.
Equality is a weapon used by Sinn Fein/IRA to wage war on every expression of British pride, sovereignty and cultural identity in Northern Ireland. This sectarian campaign also extends wider to seek the eradication of Biblical Protestantism.

This crude device is armed by legislation enacted under section 75 of the Northern Ireland Act 1998, a perverse piece of legislation that creates parity between Britishness and Irishness while demanding that the foreign identity of those who seek to destroy Northern Ireland's constitutional position must be given equal prominence alongside the National identity of those who give their loyalty to the Country!
This is a hideous abuse of the desired meaning of equality!

The Haass document highlighted the trajectory of the 'equality agenda' when it spoke of *"a special and protected place for Irishness"* and also proposed a role for the *"Sovereign flag of Ireland in conjunction with the Union flag"*.
If ever alarm bells should ring, it is now!

The equality agenda seeks to do the damage via the backdoor by using the contrived notion of 'Shared Space'. This was originally brought to the fore by the Alliance party driven Cohesion, Sharing & Integration document which was rejected. This however was not the end and the OFMDFM strategy document is now beginning to take shape.
This DUP/SF document bears all the hallmarks of the sneaky equality agenda and is ambiguous, thus granting republicanism the tools they require to ratchet their cultural war up to the next level!

Flags, Parades, bonfires, memorials to the UDR/RUC/British Army/Loyalists, the wearing of the Poppy, the 12th July public holiday and street preaching are all in Sinn Fein/IRA sights!

This agenda seeks to legislate the Protestant, Unionist & Loyalist community out of our culture and many have already agreed to things such as the following for bonfires (even though they were explicitly warned of the trajectory of such manoeuvres):

Public liability insurance for bonfires- There only needs to be one fatality or serious injury related to a bonfire and the cost for insuring the bonfire will be too much for any local community to afford, thus without the correct insurance the bonfire will be illegal, opening the door for criminalisation of bonfire builders and enforcement by the PSNI.

Protocol Agreements on the burning of foreign flags on bonfires- These agreements seek to step by step make bonfires a neutral, shared space. Of course a bonfire it itself is an expression of single identity culture and the envisaged dilution will effectively render bonfires obsolete!

The ring fencing of cultural expression with legislation such as section 75 of the Northern Ireland Act 1998 is gradually seeking to *piece by peace* dilute all expressions of single identity British, Protestant, Unionist & Loyalist culture and heritage which will eventually render them obsolete! The seeds of this agenda were planted in the Belfast/St Andrew's/Hillsborough Agreements!

OTR Scheme- the Questions that must be answered!

This document was written up by me following a meeting with the individual referred to previously in the book as X. I was shown sensitive documents that raise serious questions about the true nature of the Governments "On the runs" scheme. This document was sent to Kate Hoey MP who in turn raised some of the matters with the Secretary of State in Parliament. This result in the SOS having to admit that as well as letters of immunity, the Government had also issued Royal Pardons to IRA terrorists.

The following list of questions are those which I believe need to be answered in the course of the NI select affairs committee investigation into the heinous abuse of lawful process that took place as part of the OTR 'administrative' scheme.

1) Former RUC/PSNI officer Norman Baxter last week informed the committee that there were other examples of Sinn Fein/NIO interfering with the due process of law and order. Mr Baxter said he did not wish to go into these areas in a public forum.
I believe it is absolutely essential that the committee speak to Mr Baxter in a more suitable forum and ascertain the nature of these other instances. If there has been other attempts to pervert the course of justice by the NIO, Sinn Fein or elements of the PSNI then this must be rigorously investigated. I believe it is of the utmost importance that Mr Baxter is able to reveal this information as the earliest possible opportunity. I also believe that this information should then be very quickly made public knowledge. I find it hard to believe, in fact almost inconceivable, that the information Mr Baxter possessed would contravene the official secrets act.
The PUL community have had enough of cover ups and this area of Mr Baxter's evidence should be fully exhausted and all aspects of NIO/Sinn Fein tampering with policing exposed.

2) It seems to be the case that the files Operation RAPID 'looked over' were only intelligence files, not actual case files. It appears the RAPID team didn't collaborate the various strands of evidence in relation to particular offences to ascertain if the threshold had been met, instead due to the inner

workings of the PSNI they would have merely looked over intelligence files on named individuals. If, as I believe is the case, the administrative scheme merely looked over intelligence files on individuals then surely the British Government should rescind the letters and collaborate all the evidence for offences and look again to see if these individuals can be prosecuted.

3) The committee should pay particular attention to the involvement of Mr Barra McGrory, current head of the PPS for NI, in the OTR scheme. I believe it is vitally important to find out if Mr McGrory declared his involvement in this scheme prior to taking up the post of DPP and if he did not, why not? The confidence in the impartiality of the PPS is at an all time low and it is essential that the committee investigates exactly what role Mr McGrory played and whether this was declared upon his appointment as DPP.

4) It is also important to ascertain whether current Northern Ireland Attorney General John Larkin had any involvement in the OTR scheme. Mr Larkin provided legal advice to Sinn Fein and also to the DUP during negotiations around the St Andrews & Hillsborough Agreements. If Mr Larkin was aware of the existence of the OTR scheme, did this colour his judgement in any decisions he has since made in his role of Attorney General? It is also vital to explore whether Mr Larkin declared any involvement in the OTR negotiations/scheme prior to taking up his role as Attorney General.

5) In relation to both questions 4 & 5 it is only logical to now investigate what procedures the NIO put in place for the OTR scheme when John Larkin and Barra McGrory came into post. Given Mr McGrory's involvement and quite possibly also John Larkin's, surely the NIO and those behind the scheme would have had guidelines in place to prevent a conflict of interest arising in dealing with the OTR's?

6) Did the NIO or any other organisation involved in the OTR scheme authorise, facilitate or actively participate in the setting up of a pension scheme for those who had been OTR?

7) Did the NIO or any other organisation involved in the OTR scheme authorise, facilitate or actively participate in providing compensation to any of the OTR'S?

8) Was a Royal Pardon given to any Sinn Fein members? If this is the case, as I believe it is, then what were the guidelines for administrating these pardons and were elected officials and members of Sinn Fein treated more favourably than ordinary citizens?

9) I am led to believe historical case files meet the evidence threshold in relation to a number of senior Sinn Fein members yet these cases are not being progressed. Did any Senior Sinn Fein members receive any kind of variation of the 'comfort letters' granting them immunity from prosecution?

10) Mr Norman Baxter spoke of a phone call from the duty ACC advising him to release two IRA terrorists arrested for the attempted murder of UDR soldier Mr Sammy Brush. It is important to ask why this duty ACC was not reported and investigated for attempting to pervert the course of justice. Did Sir Hugh Orde have any agreement with the NIO in relation to the progression of cases against Republicans and what terms of reference were agreed between the NIO and senior command of the PSNI in relation to Operation RAPID? It is entirely unreasonable to think that the NIO would have requested the PSNI to undertake such a task and if the PSNI had indentified evidence to arrest OTR's that they would have then been allowed to do so. There has been some level of 'understanding' between Sinn Fein, the NIO and the PSNI about the process in relation to scheme.

11) How many OTR's are still wanted following the completion/suspension of Operation RAPID? It is somewhat ludicrous to suggest that of all the IRA OTR's, many of whom the RUC/PSNI had actively sought because the evidence threshold met the required level to arrest, are now not wanted. Are we really expected to believe that all the original evidence, against all the OTR's, is now all of a sudden inadmissible or does not meet the evidence threshold?

12) were the HET investigating any of the individuals who received comfort letters and as a result how many HET case files were closed?

13) Did the NIO implement any similar schemes to ensure that the highest echelons of the Sinn Fein leadership received immunity from prosecution? This could have been in the form of Pardons or some other contrived NIO circumvention of the judicial process. To get to the truth of this matter it is important to find out from the PSNI whether they were tasked to 'look over' the intelligence files on any senior Sinn Fein members who were not on the run and what subsequently happened with these files? I am reliably informed that the committee will find that intelligence files and evidence that implicated the most senior Sinn Fein members in acts of terrorism were destroyed following the St Andrews agreement.

14) Were the British Security forces running agents at the very top of Sinn Fein? Were these individuals also allowed to bypass the judicial process and did MI5/M16 put pressure on the NIO to implement this scheme?

15) Norman Baxter was the PSNI liaison with MI5. Mr Baxter said that he feared 'some people' would attempt to hang him out to dry over the OTR scheme. Did MI5 put pressure on Norman Baxter to ensure that various republicans that were not OTR, but were 'assets' also received effective immunity? It is important that Norman Baxter is protected and is asked and is given the opportunity to answer these questions without fear of reprisals from various arms of the British Security forces.

16) Was the Royal Prerogative of Mercy issued as part of the OTR scheme or as part of any agreement between Sinn Fein and the British Government?

17) Were any of those who received Royal Pardons working as paid informers for British Intelligence services?

The above questions need to be answered. The continued cover up must be uncovered and I hope that the NI select affairs committee will be the body to uncover the much deeper secret that lurks beneath the surface of the Peace Process.
If answered, the questions will open the doors to exposing the most horrid abuses of law and justice and indeed the 'secret' Agreements made under the table during the devolution of policing and justice. This goes right to the heart of the appointments of Mr John Larkin as AG and Barra McGrory as DPP.

It is also a terrible hidden truth that senior Sinn Fein members received immunity from prosecution and a secret operation took place within the corridors of the NIO & PSNI to 'lose' evidence against them.

The intelligence files may remain, the evidence however will not. It has been destroyed as part of the much wider scheme, a scheme that dwarfs the scandal of the 'Administrative scheme'.

The scheme not only dealt with OTR's but also with senior Sinn Fein elected officials. Justice was betrayed so as to protect the process.

The end of freedom

In recent times the Protestant people of Ulster have suffered greatly as a result of the violence inflicted upon them by violent republican terrorists.

Today the people of Ulster suffer at the hands of legislation implemented as a result of the failed Good Friday Agreement which creates a state where your freedoms of civil and religious liberty are slowly stripped away under the auspices of 'legislation'. The people then feel out of a sense of being loyal law abiding citizens that they must obey these unjust laws, created so as to appease the very people whose aim is the destruction of the state the so called peace process has given them an enormous say over.

Following the tearing down of the Union flag from the capital city a number of people who have engaged in peaceful protest have seen the evil underbelly of this process manifest itself in the abuse of laws and legislation, so as to quell any opposition to the injustice that is so rife in Ulster today.

The weapon of choice to implement these unjust laws is the PSNI, a police force which was meant to be impartial yet has provided so many concessions and seeks to appease the mainstream republican movement so much that they have emancipated themselves from the law abiding Protestant people, who's rights they trample over and who's identity they seek to oppress at the behest of Sinn Fein/IRA.

As part of the GFA it was agreed that there should be a parades commission, whose weapon would be the PSNI and this so called commission would adjudicate on matters pertaining to public processions. It is a widely agreed point that the parades commission have failed miserably and as a result of the recent flag protests, their legitimacy and authority has been diminished to the point of irrelevance and this has created a vacuum in which the PSNI can 'interpret' legislation in whichever way they choose and indeed abuse legislation when they require an excuse to oppress ones free speech and freedom of political thought and expression.

The PSNI have recently charged a number of peaceful protests for 'taking part in a un notified public procession' and have also used the serious crime act 2007 section 46 'encouraging or assisting offences'. The offences those charges are charged with assisting? Unnotified Public processions.

To begin to understand these oppressive laws one must look at why they were designed. The serious crime act section 46 was designed so as to give the authorities in England some way of dealing with radical Muslim hate preachers. The PSNI have used this legislation to deal with those preaching 'peaceful protest' and claimed those arrested have encouraged 'public processions'.

It is a person's basic human right to engage in peaceful protest, however the PSNI have managed to create a loophole in which they can squash this human right but dress it up under 'catch all' legislation which basically allows them to lock up anyone who's political views may not be beneficial to the current political climate. The PSNI can squash free speech and peaceful protest by using legislation and thus criminalise anyone whose political views they or the state for whom they act, disapprove. It is a modern weapon for the PSNI to intern easily anyone who speaks out against a failing system. As this is an indictable offence and thus on the face of it PSNI can present it as 'serious crime', they have a reasonable chance of ensuring those they wish to intern are refused bail.

In this case one whose political views are disapproved off by the system can be criminalised and demonised. It is important however to note that obeying these unjust laws makes one unjust themselves.

In regards to the public procession, the PSNI have charged people under Section 6 of the public processions act 1998. It is interesting to note however that the legislation, which is effectively the law, provides no definition whatsoever in relation to what actually constitutes a 'procession'. It is understood that those charged have been subject to the PSNI interpretation of what a 'procession' is and thus this has no basis in law. This has allowed the PSNI too effectively to decide the law, whilst there is actually no legislation to back up this law and then intern persons on the basis of it. That is a dangerous situation whereas we have a state police force who without legislative or lawful authority can place their definition on acts and decide willy nilly whether they want them to be legal or not, without any judicial clarity.

The 1998 public processions act section 17- 1 (b) defines a public procession *as 'a procession in a public place'.* This leaves no clarity on what actually constitutes a procession. The PSNI have said that they would use the Oxford dictionary for definitions of acts where there is no legislative clarity (it is unclear whether this is PSNI policy or just the policy of certain officers, clarity must also be sought on this matter.)

The Oxford dictionary defines a 'procession' as *'a number of people or Vehicles moving forward in an orderly fashion'*. This however provides no clarity on what the public processions act 1998 actually covers in terms of processions. Where there is no legislative definition surely it is totally flying in the face of democracy to allow a police force to make their definition up on the basis of what suits the political climate of the time?

Legally the PSNI have interned and charged a number of persons not on the basis of legislative law, but on the basis of their interpretation of that law. This creates a very serious issue within a so called democratic society and effectively removes the power from the democratic system and places it in the hands of a police force who are accountable to a policing board which contains former terrorists and known subversives.

The 50-50 recruitment concession the IRA managed to get as a result of the destruction of the RUC and the formation of the PSNI raises concerns as to the impartiality of our police force should they continue to be given a free hand to enforce order without law.

The PSNI have defined a 'procession' as 3 or more persons moving with a common purpose, either on a public road or a footpath'. Again to be clear this has no legislative authority and therefore should not be viewed as 'law'. With this in mind the PSNI have been effectively able to enforce 'marshal law' in regards to the Protestant community. This definition however, under which the PSNI have charged many people using this as their 'evidence threshold' leaves the door open for serious restrictions to be put on all citizens and indeed once again gives the PSNI a free hand to pick and choose who they want to arrest.

If for example a family of 3 are walking along the footpath all heading for a meal, under the PSNI definition these persons are meeting the evidence threshold for what is a 'procession'. These 3 persons are walking with a common purpose and would have not notified the parades commission. As each person is supposed to be equally subject to the law and equal under the law, what criteria do the PSNI use when deciding when persons are going to be arrested for their definition of a procession? As is abundantly clear the PSNI have now taken it upon them to set themselves up as judge and jury and they have the power to decide what is and what a procession isn't. This is a serious equality issue under the European law of Human rights.

How can one person be subject to a law in one instance and another person have impunity?

For years when football matches have been played fans walk with a common purpose to the ground in large numbers and indeed still do on a weekly basis. This by the PSNI definition they have used as their evidence threshold in charging persons is a procession yet not once have they made any arrests? As I am sure one can see clearly from this short analysis it is very dangerous where we have a police force that can place their definition on legislation and furthermore decide where this definition applies and to whom it applies. This is not even handing policing and it allows, as we have seen, the oppression of peaceful protest, expressions of political thought, free speech and civil and religious liberty.

As it is a cornerstone of British democracy that a law cannot be created and a person charged retrospectively surely it therefore is clear that the PSNI, acting outside and without legal clarity, interned a number of law abiding British citizens in an attempt to criminalise them and squash the democratic right of peaceful opposition to the government. This clearly demonstrates that there must be an urgent review of the PSNI and how they implement law in Northern Ireland.

There is a clear bias towards the Nationalist community which has been clearly demonstrated over the course of peaceful protests and indeed as Nationalists where given freedom to burn the Union flag and celebrate on the streets taking part in many unnotified processions with impunity.

Is it a case that it is a 'crime' for one community and totally acceptable for another in the eyes of the PSNI?

This bias has also been clear in the PSNI approach to bail, whilst PSNI agree to bail in the case of convicted Republican terrorists they oppose bail strenuously in the case of peaceful protestors. To whose agenda are they working?

It is understandable that there is a palpable sense of confusion within the PUL community and indeed it is hardly surprising that the view that a unjust law is no law at all, is beginning to prevail amidst the fact that legislatively there effectively is no definition as to what constitutes a procession and the PSNI are creating laws to suit each occasion, by adding their definition onto whatever legislation best suits. It's a case of a square peg in a round hole in regards to the PSNI's use of legislation.

If indeed there is no definition then surely the parades commission are irrelevant and unless the PSNI are going to operate with the same policy overall and judicial clarity is given over what is a procession, then either every single group of more than 3 people walking any distance at all must submit to the parades commission or no one must submit. The law must treat all equally so unless the public processions act 1998 is amended to provide clarity there is almost no way of doing this, so it is only fair to assume that no notification should be given until there is a legislative definition as to what constitutes a procession and thus the PSNI have no legal authority to arrest and charge without legislation to back up their charges (a definition they have concocted does not suffice) so anyone detained by the PSNI in regards to processions is actually unlawfully detained because there is no clear legislation to determine what a procession is.

For God And Ulster

Traditional Loyalism in modern society

I have been greatly disturbed by a small but significant number of loyalists attempting to fundamentally alter the founding elements of traditional loyalism in the name of 'evolving' or 'modernising'. This has ranged from a subtle but significant separation between God and our cause with many taking the view that Bible believing Protestantism should be kept separate from the cause of loyalism.

There has also been a rise in extreme socialist and liberal politics which is anathema to the reformed faith of Protestantism.

The natural home of Loyalism is within Bible based Protestantism; it is this faith that has provided the moral and spiritual backbone to our cause for generations. It is from this reformed faith that sprang the motto *'For God And Ulster'* that is proudly carried on our standards and engraved upon our murals and headstones all over this Country.

Attempts to pursue political or social aims that quite clearly undermine the word of God subsequently cast a dark shadow over the religious element of our cause.

It is an indisputable fact that the majority of those within loyalism would not be practising Protestants however it is important to keep in focus the moral and social stability that is provided from a continued reliance on Biblical principles.

Aside from the religious side of things, the attempts to dilute loyalism to become a 'please everyone all of time' modern liberal identity is the very thing that will sow the seeds of the ultimate destruction of the loyalist identity.

The attempts to re-brand loyalism into some kind of ultra accepting, liberal identity of appeasement and compromise with a strong reliance on extreme left wing politics will perhaps attract some young 'hug the world' type of voters, it will however more tellingly alienate the core base of traditional loyalists, many of whom whilst being a long way from practising Protestants, would still draw strongly on moral Biblical principles and would still argue fiercely for the merits of Protestantism and faith in God underpinning our cause.

The Bible believing section of loyalism would be described as 'intransigent dinosaurs who are bigots, sectarian and homophobic' to name but a few tags that would be thrown towards us.

These words play to one of the fundamental truths of communication, words matter.

The use of these words has an automatic stigma, an automatic turn off affect in the minds of the majority of the population.

The truth of the matter is that it is very easy to throw these labels towards people who refuse to compromise their core beliefs. It is an easy way to discredit political arguments that do not embrace the 'hug the world' attitude. It is a favourite tactic of liberals and socialists.

There is no shame in refusing to compromise your core beliefs and there is no merit in diluting or changing your cultural or religious identity so as to ensure you offend no one or to appease those that wish to force change upon you. Many men fought and died 'For God And Ulster' and it is proudly carried on many of our modern and traditional standards. A political move away from the social principles of God's word towards a liberal and socialist doctrine of removing all traces of God from politics and society in general is a move that will provide for nothing but disaster.

A brand of loyalism that seeks to separate God from politics has little that separates it from extreme socialism and given that I would contend that Sinn Fein and the SDLP are both Nationalist Socialists, when you take away the constitutional issue and cultural issues (which most of the tree huggers will readily compromise if they are forced to in the name of 'equality') then there is very little that will separate the new brand of 'loyalist' from those who seek to destroy our Country.

They will find common cause in extreme left wing politics which will remove every trace of Godly principles from society, schools and Government and eventually provide the destruction of the stable communities and society that have served the United Kingdom so well for Centuries. The strong foundations of biblical principles will be removed in exchange for an atheist 'anything goes' society without parameters or boundaries and where everything that anybody says makes them happy is accepted in the perverse name of 'equality'.

This type of 'Unionism' has already been seen in all its glory with Basil McCrea and his NI21 party. This is the trajectory of attempts to liberalise loyalism and shift it sharply to the left of the political spectrum.

The traditional 'loyalism' and 'Unionism' was strong and uncompromising. It was based and relied heavily upon biblical and Godly principles.

The Solemn League and Covenant which has been often described as the Birth certificate of Northern Ireland placed strong emphasis on many principles of the reformed Protestant faith.

Contrary to recent assertions the majority of the signatories of the Ulster Covenant would not have been left wing socialists but instead working class centre right Bible believing Protestants.

The attempt to turn a solemn promise to strive for 'Civil and Religious liberty' into a weapon to be used in campaigns to undermine God's word under the cloak of equality is a perverse and gross miss-interpretation of the original meaning.

Does anyone seriously contend that those who framed the Covenant would have in any way supported undermining Gods word in the name of 'equality'? This Covenant was drawn up by those steadfast and resolute in their commitment to the reformed faith and therefore the Civil and Religious liberty they spoke of was not to be taken as 'anything goes as long as it makes people happy'. It has to be taken in the Christian context in which it was written.

The anchor of loyalism has always been the 'For God' element based within Bible believing Protestantism which has provided a stable backbone to the Loyalist cause.

This is not to say that every loyalist even believes in God, but the majority would have some resemblance of Protestant faith, especially older generations.

The argument I make is that if loyalism abandons the word of God then it abandons everything we stand for and it abandons the fundamental principles that our forefathers fought and died for.

In one recent example a loyalist said to me 'Yes but when you are saying For God And Ulster you just mean your God, what about all the other Gods?' This is an example of how the liberalising of loyalism could lead to a frightening dilution of our identity.

Entwined within Loyalism is Protestantism. To crystallise the point I am making, the attempts to create a liberal socialist Loyalism will seek to separate loyalism from Protestantism. This would depart from everything that our forefathers fought and died to maintain.

To stay true to our founding principles we must stay true to the genuine principles of the Ulster Covenant and robustly challenge any attempts to dilute them or 'evolve' them to suit modern whims.

Loyalism does not need to move forward any further, we need to go back to what loyalism really is and what it always has been. It is based in the Protestant faith and it carries the motto For God and Ulster.

Stay true to who we really are.

FOR GOD AND ULSTER

Traditional Loyalism in Modern Society-A response to Richard Reed

The following article was written in response to academic Richard Reed on the Long Kesh inside out website. Mr Reed had submitted a highly critical response to my "For God And Ulster-Traditional Loyalism in Modern Society" piece.

I wish to respond to an article submitted by Richard Reed to the Long Kesh site regarding my subject 'Traditional Loyalism in Modern Society.'

Mr Reed's article has been re-tweeted by those that would seem keen to endorse his view.

A point was made to me at the weekend during a good-natured debate around gay marriage which I indeed accept to be true, namely that no one policy defines a Party. By the same token no one viewpoint defines a person. Mr Reed seems to have missed this fundamental truth by directing his comments as a poor attempt to defame my character and undermine my argument.

Mr Reed spends a lot of literary effort attempting to separate traditional Protestant values from modern Loyalism, and to be frank, I believe he provides a poor theological basis for this.

His argument woven through the article is that he suggests Protestantism, which separated initially from Catholicism, (reformation period) should somehow move with the times and 'evolve' is a bizarre and illogical argument when presented on a Biblical basis.

The reformers 'protested' against the teachings and non-Biblical interpretations of the Catholic Church, and they indeed did give birth to what has become known as the Protestant Reformation which has evolved to this very day as the only sound biblical defender of the faith.

I understand Mr Reed's point (although I fail to agree with him on it) that social identities must evolve, however to do this he contends that Loyalism must completely separate from Protestantism to survive and play a role in 'modern' society. Or this would seem to be the logical outcome of his argument.

It is my belief Protestantism can only evolve based upon sound Biblical principles, for indeed it's foundation is grounded in the infallible, inerrant

word of God and is unchanging for all eternity. To therefore ask Protestantism to liberalise or modernize is a nonsense because as stated, it is founded upon the unchanging the word of God.
Mr Reed asks the question, "What is God's Word?

I believe the word of God is what is written in the Bible. As Jesus himself (Who is the Word of God incarnate) says 'It is written'.
Mr Reed's response at times shifts the initial debate into another sphere around the founding principles of Protestantism and on into a much deeper theological discussion. In essence I believe that Mr Reed's commentary on this particular section is theologically incorrect and is a misinterpretation of the reformation and glorious Protestant revolution. The reformers based their social principles on Biblical principles. They did not break away from the word of God; they broke away from a Church that claimed divine right to interpret the word of God.

Their argument was on a human not a spiritual level. Their 'uprising' was not against God, but against the Catholic Church which had forsaken the word of God.

This brings us to the argument that clearly arises following my original piece and Mr Reed's response, 'Does Loyalism need to create an identity without the 'shackles' of the Biblical principles that comes with Protestantism?'

My original piece clearly contends that Loyalism is best served by maintaining Biblical principles.

Mr Reed's argument suggests that Loyalism needs to embrace social change and liberalise views on social issues.

But the views and positions taken politically by many sections of Loyalism are based on a personal Protestant faith founded on the Word of God. It is an indisputable fact that for a wide section of Loyalism, their personal Protestant faith serves as a root for their Loyalist identity.

It is now however an ideological argument developing within Loyalism around what the anchors of loyalist identity actually are. This is being played out in the political sphere.

In previous eras differences such as the (GFA) Yes/No campaign and the breakaway of Loyalist groups who were opposed to the embryonic Peace Process were based upon differences around engagement in the political process.

Today's debates centre around what political and social positions should shape the Loyalist ideology in the context of participation in this political process.

The problem is there are so many different and complex social and political positions amongst Loyalism that it is difficult to present a political manifesto that will act as a core ideological position on Loyalism. This, I believe, is the root cause of Loyalism's internal political disagreements.

Mr Reed dismisses out of hand the position taken up by those who share my viewpoint. In contrast to Mr Reed's view, I recognise the position of various elements of Loyalism that base their idea of Loyalism around a different interpretation / ideology and who indeed interpret the Covenant of 1912 and our historical 'cause' in many different ways.

I have previously made my case around my beliefs, however I am conscious of the differences in viewpoint and am prepared to ask the difficult questions that need answered if intra loyalist unity is to be efficiently achieved in the context of building an effective political base.

In this context Mr Reed has initiated a debate around very difficult and emotive questions that admittedly will be difficult to answer and has created an environment for extremely complex debates.

Based on Mr Reeds response and the numerous contradictory elements within Loyalism today, is it wrong to ask is Loyalism an identity in itself or is it a 'name tag' created to describe a wide range of different identities?

If it is the former (an identity in itself) then a debate must take place around what is actually the natural ideological position of Loyalism. Is it rooted in Biblical Protestantism or not? If as I believe it fundamentally is, then Loyalism must stay true to the motto 'For God and Ulster' or 'In God Our Trust' and base political and social positions around this.

If it isn't (founded in Protestantism) then Loyalism must separate itself from Biblical principles.

If it is the latter ('a name tag' created to describe a wide range of different identities) then Loyalism must shape a common identity that will find common ideological ground between the often-contradictory sections of Loyalism.

In the context of this response to Mr Reed I have simply attempted to highlight the questions that need to be answered. I have attempted to move the debate to a different level.

It is clear and evident that a wide section of Loyalism would agree with my initial piece and an equally wide section would subscribe to the viewpoint presented by Mr Reed.

This draws the 'battle lines' for the debate that Loyalism needs to have and as one person said to me recently, "Every battle ends around the table". The core aim must be getting the debate around the table before it becomes a publicly played out political war of words that will only serve to play into the hands of Republicanism and the clear systemic problems that emanate from our system of Government in Northern Ireland.

Who Judges the Judges?

Nb. This document is an account that was given to me by a reliable source a number of years ago.

The Consultative Group on the Past is an independent group established to consult across the community in Northern Ireland on the best way to deal with the legacy of the Troubles.

The Group states its terms of reference as:

"To consult across the community on how Northern Ireland society can best approach the legacy of the events of the past 40 years; and to make recommendations, as appropriate, on any steps that might be taken to support Northern Ireland society in building a shared future that is not overshadowed by the events of the past."

With these terms of reference as a starting point let me begin to tell a story..........

In 1972 in County Londonderry three car bombs were placed at intervals along Claudy town's High Street, which was busy with shoppers at the time of the attack. The attack killed six people immediately, with three later dying from their injuries. A young girl and two teenage boys were among the dead. Five of the victims were Catholic, and four were Protestant.

These bombs had been prepared at the house of 'Bomber Blew' in Bellaghy, County Londonderry, about five miles from Magherafelt. The deadly cargo was loaded and driven to Desertmartin village and left overnight at the local GAA club. (Gaelic Athletic Association)

The next morning the bombs were driven to Claudy by three men, one of whom was local parish priest Father James Chesney (Deceased) who was later accused of being the leader of the Claudy attack and was himself a member of the South Derry Brigade of the Provisional IRA.

Father Chesney did drive to Dungiven to give a warning about the bombs but the PIRA had earlier taken out the telephone system, thus no warning could be given.

This information came to light after an IRA man contacted Ivan Cooper Member of the Parliament of Northern Ireland, and founding member of the SDLP. He related everything about the Claudy bombing and who was involved. The IRA man then went to Maghera RUC Station and confessed what he had told Ivan Cooper. Superintendent Frank Lagan was called to investigate the claims made.

At the same time British Intelligence sources were operating throughout County Londonderry as 'Operation Motorman' was underway to re-establish control of areas that had become 'no go areas,' and their information told them that if the Ulster Defence Association (UDA) were made aware a parish priest was involved in the Claudy atrocity they (UDA) would consider all Catholic priests 'legitimate targets' and UDA leaders would issue orders to their personnel to eliminate such without conscience. This could not be allowed to happen and so the British Prime Minister Edward Heath ordered William Whitelaw Secretary of State for Northern Ireland to find a solution to the difficulty.

Superintendent Frank Lagan contacted Father Denis Bradley as he was known as the official 'go-between' for the Catholic Church and the PIRA in Londonderry. Superintendent Lagan had on numerous occasions got Father Denis Bradley to contact the PIRA about his officers being targeted. Now Bradley would become the 'go-between' for the RUC and the PIRA. He made contact with Martin McGuinness (currently Deputy First Minister of Northern Ireland) who in turn immediately contacted Sean Mac-Stiofain (born John Edward Drayton Stephenson) the then Chief of Staff of the Provisional IRA. Meetings were organised which took place in Donegal and were attended by Northern Ireland Office representatives and Martin McGuinness (who would eventually take over command of the PIRA in Derry.)

Martin McGuinness was afforded free passage to and from the meetings as RUC officers and British Army patrols were ordered 'not to stop his vehicle.'

One outcome of these secret meetings was the PIRA would not claim responsibility for the Claudy attack and the British government would also say there was 'no intelligence suggesting IRA involvement.'

One week after these meetings took place William Whitelaw met with Cardinal Conway to discuss the Claudy bombings at which Whitelaw demanded from the Catholic leader that the British government in future could request any priest or bishop could be moved from a particular diocese. Cardinal Conway agreed! One week after the meeting investigations into the Claudy atrocity were closed.

Shortly after this Father James Chesney was moved to a new parish in Muff, County Donegal and Father Denis Bradley felt a 'strong urge' having met a woman, to leave the priesthood. Within only a short period William Whitelaw, Cardinal William Conway, Superintendent Frank Lagan and Bishop Farren all retired or withdrew from public life and duties due to illness.

The Consultative Group on the Past which includes Bishop Robin Eames and former (Father) Denis Bradley was established to consult across the community in Northern Ireland on the best way to deal with the legacy of the Troubles, 'and to make recommendations, as appropriate, on any steps that might be taken to support Northern Ireland society in building a shared future that is not overshadowed by the events of the past.'

There are many people who should tell the truth about their own involvement in atrocities such as Claudy.

In light of the authorities that have been involved in covering up these truths, do you seriously think that even an inquiry would give us the truth?

To help build a shared future for all the citizens of Northern Ireland, one that is not overshadowed by the events of the past, I recommend we all ask ourselves, "Who judges the Judges?"

In this account all but Bradley and McGuinness are deceased but this should not deter any proper investigation, in fact should all the more encourage one.

Who Judges the Judges- Part Two

Nb. This document is an account that was given to me by a reliable source a number of years ago.

In light of the Claudy developments it would be remiss of me not to offer further information as had been promised. Even though our Deputy First Minister was never so thankful so have the Billy Wright Inquiry Report launched to remove the pressure and the world spotlight from him and his role within the Claudy atrocity, I would just like to inform him in the words of his comrade, "We haven't gone away you know!"

Here's the next piece of the jigsaw which we believe will help put together the whole picture of the Claudy cover up between the British Government, the Roman Catholic Church, the IRA's Martin McGuinness, Denis Bradley, Father James Chesney and others.

The Claudy bombs as we have stated earlier (Who Judges the Judges 1) were produced by Bomber (Blew) Blue in Bellaghy and were driven by James Chesney and his cohorts to Desertmartin GAA grounds and stored there overnight before being taken the next day to Claudy.

When the bombs exploded and the evil deeds' victims counted, the British Government rapidly arranged to meet with Superintendant Frank Lagan and Father Denis Bradley and asked them to arrange a meeting with the IRA.

The first of a number of meetings took place in Donegal to which Martin McGuinness as the negotiator appointed by Chief of Staff of the IRA Sean MacStiofain was given free passage to attend. MacStiofan would shortly relinquish command of the whole of Derry and commit it to Martin McGuinness.

The agreement negotiated was this:

1) The IRA would not claim the Claudy bombing because if the UDA found out a priest was involved they would order their personnel to go out and shoot priests "without conscience."
2) The British Government could ask the Bishop of any diocese to remove any priest from that diocese if he was suspected of paramilitary activity or child sexual abuse.

Having done this deal within days the Claudy atrocity file was subsequently closed and made to look like the RUC had not compiled enough evidence to point the blame at any particular organisation, thus belittling the RUC officers in charge of the investigation and covering up any forensic evidence they may have had to the contrary. But let's just look at a couple of facts.

On December 18th 1971 Martin Lee (18yrs), John Bateson (18yrs) and James Sheridan (19yrs) were ordered by their commanding officer Father James Chesney to deliver a bomb to Magherafelt town centre, prime it and leave it to explode. However the bomb went off prematurely and the three terrorists were killed. RUC officers and forensics were quickly on the scene gathering vital evidence.

In February (6th) 1972 Phelim Grant (from the North Antrim brigade of the IRA which worked closely with the South Derry brigade) and Charles McCann (Toomebridge) both IRA men were ordered by the commanding officer Father James Chesney to deliver a bomb to the sand barges in Lough Neagh. Yet again this bomb went off prematurely outside Crumlin killing all three terrorists. Once again the RUC officers and forensics were on the scene gathering up the shrapnel for further analysis.

Then in July 1972 the Claudy atrocity was carried out.

The head of the RUC at the time in South Londonderry area was Superintendant Frank Lagan who publicly stated there was no evidence to suggest the IRA carried out the Claudy attack, however forensic evidence clearly shows the same bomb manufacturer who made the previous bombs for the IRA (Magherafelt / Crumlin) without doubt also made the bombs that caused havoc in Claudy. Now the question to be asked is why was this information not given out to the general public?

Bomber (Blew) Blue from Bellaghy (an IRA member) made each of the six bombs used in the incidents mentioned (1 Magherafelt, 1 Crumlin and 3 Claudy) and was under the direct command of Father James Chesney who was under the command of one Mr Martin McGuinness. This proves without doubt the IRA carried out the Claudy bombing.

Is it not time for the IRA to tell the truth and for Martin McGuinness to admit his role. Also the Reverend William McCrea was fully aware of the cover up of the Claudy atrocity having held a meeting with 'influential' men at the rear of his Church to discuss using parliamentary privilege to name those in authority behind the bombing campaign but he answered (verbatim) *"We don't want to embarrass the British government at this time."*

This information is available within the annals of the forensic science laboratories and RUC intelligence should be released to the wider public.

A simple call to the Reverend William McCrea will also confirm his knowledge.

If as the Association of former Police Officers suggests the Claudy investigation should be re-opened then evidence such as this should not be forgotten or hidden away to cover up the cover up composed by the British Government, the Roman Catholic Church, the IRA's Martin McGuinness, Denis Bradley, Father James Chesney and others.

In the midst of all of this subterfuge let's not forget the victims of Claudy, for it is they who have suffered the most.

Police Ombudsman Complaint

This document contains two sections of complaints in relation to serious PSNI misconduct.
This includes serious crime, abuses of lawful process, facilitation of illegal acts for political expediency and perjury in the Court of Law.

A copy of this document will be released into the public domain as I believe it is essential that the general public are aware of the underhand tactics deployed by our police force and to also act as a safety net against the inevitable Government and security forces sinister attempts to whitewash any investigations.

This document will be presented in full to the Police Ombudsman for NI, members of the Policing board, the media and the Secretary of State for NI.

By Jamie Bryson

*A number of names and personal details have been redacted from this document.

1) Complaints arising from the facilitation of weekly walks from City Hall to East Belfast and vice versa.

Complaints overview:

(A) It is my complaint that the PSNI engaged the assistance of community representatives in relation to weekly walks on 12th & 19th January 2013 and knowingly encouraged the re-routing of aforementioned walks. The PSNI now claim these walks were something which they knew to be illegal, and later arrested with the view to prosecution participants in the walks that took place on 12th & 19th January. They did not inform those they engaged with that the walks were illegal and in fact they actually publicly stated that *"there is no such thing as an illegal parade under the public processions act"*.
The legal contention of this part of my complaint is that the PSNI engaged in Entrapment and are criminally liable under **Section 46 of the Serious Crime Act 2007** 'encouraging or assisting offences believing one or more will be committed.'

(B) It is my complaint that it was an act of serious misconduct by the PSNI to engage in meetings with myself and other named representatives of the UPF and discuss the facilitation of walks which they knew to be illegal, but failed to define as such. At the time of these meetings one or more of the talk's participants were under criminal investigation for offences linked to the Union flag dispute. Despite this the PSNI issued a media statement praising the UPF.

(C) It is my complaint that a decision was taken within high levels of the PSNI command structure to arrest me based not upon substantive evidence (as has been proven by the PPS withdrawal of the charges) but upon the need to remove and silence someone who was destabilising the political process and who the PSNI needed removed from the equation so as to give other Civic leaders who were more sympathetic to the PSNI position breathing space to change the tempo and direction of the Union flag protests.

(D) It is my complaint that during a meeting between Gerry Kelly MLA as part of a Sinn Fein delegation and Chief Constable Matt Baggott on 26th February 2007, a decision was taken to arrest me the following morning. On the basis of this I request the PONI investigates any communication from Senior police to the DULCET team on the night of 26th February 2013 or the early morning of 27th February 2013 and assesses whether a decision was taken and passed down to arrest me after the completion of the meeting with Sinn Fein on the evening of 26th February.

(E) It is my complaint that the Chief Constable placed my life in danger. This relates to the meeting between the Chief Constable of the PSNI and the Sinn Fein delegation which contained a number of convicted terrorists. This meeting took place on 26th February 2013.
I believe that the PSNI breached data protection laws by discussing me and possible methods of dealing with me during the meeting with Sinn Fein.
I believe this was entirely inappropriate and a serious act of misconduct by the Chief Constable.

Background to complaints under this section:

The background to these particular allegations is the PSNI in my view attempt to ride two horses in terms of enforcing the law when it is politically expedient and when it isn't politically viable they have began granting immunity, without legislative or judicial authority, by turning a blind eye to the commission of an offence or offences when it is deemed to be for the "greater good."
   This goes to the core of the debate around what legitimate role the PSNI should actually hold within our society and whether, as I contend, they have stepped over and beyond their role and into the territory of a kangaroo court granting immunity to crime if it is politically expedient.
   There are also serious questions to be asked around the PSNI use of informers and whether these self serving individuals are actually helping to fight crime or are instead being granted immunity to carry out crime in return for using any influence they have to direct a certain political agenda.
   I have watched with horror at how the PSNI abuse legislation to silence political dissent if seems more beneficial to the maintenance of stable political institutions.

I must stress, as I did within the introduction, that I firmly believe that both loyalist and republican activists that hold an anti-agreement political viewpoints are the target for these campaigns of persecution and subsequently both loyalists and republicans that are pro-agreement are the beneficiaries of it. Within this document I will deal with the issues arising from my personal loyalist perspective however I do believe that it is a vital democratic principle that all persons should be equal under the law and equally subject to the law.

The PSNI have surrounded themselves with a veil and called it 'common sense policing.' When used properly and lawfully the PSNI have every right to pursue such a strategy. This strategy has however been abused and the veil of common sense policing has become an iron curtain.
It is used to hide from the general public the bending and quite often breaking of the law for political purposes and to quash political dissent.

Complaint 1

(A)

The PSNI during the Union flag protests of 2012/13 engaged in a number of "quiet conversations" with representatives of the loyalist community. Many of these conversations were legitimate engagement with the community.
   Throughout the month of January 2013 the PSNI approached community representatives and asked them to help in the facilitation of the weekly walk from City Hall to East Belfast. The police did not advise any of the community representatives that this walk would later be termed as 'illegal' and all those participating would be subject to arrest. Instead the PSNI discussed the facilitation of various different routes that would minimise the possibility of the parade being attacked by the Nationalist Short Strand area.

Community representatives discussed these proposals with representatives of the Ulster People's Forum and other groups and asked for public support in moves to change the route of the weekly walk so as to minimise the possibility of violence.

In the first area of my complaint the PSNI held meetings on the afternoon of Friday 11th January and the morning of Saturday 12th January 2013 with a number of community and political representatives to discuss the plans for the forthcoming Saturday walk from East Belfast to City Hall and its return.

The PSNI later charged a number of the participants for taking part in an illegal procession on this date. This would suggest that the PSNI knew what they were facilitating and actively participating in the organisation of was illegal. This would constitute criminal liability under Section 46 of the Serious Crime Act 2007.

The PSNI cannot contend that they were responding to a fluid public order situation and thus justify their facilitation of the walk as a necessity. The PSNI actively engaged in the organisation of the walk at least 24 hours prior to its commencement therefore clearly they are criminally liable.

The PSNI at these meetings on 11th and 12th January 2013 sought to secure the agreement of those walking from City Hall to East Belfast that they would walk via Middlepath street and onto the Newtwownards Road from that direction. This agreement was given and the PSNI were to advise their TSG units on the ground accordingly.

This again shows that the PSNI have played a significant role in negotiations around the commissioning of something they later defined as a criminal offence.

A somewhat farcical crossing of wires within the PSNI command structure led to the blocking of the Queens Bridge by the TSG units which forced the protestors to turn right down Oxford Street.

This route led to a sustained attack from Nationalists for which the Chief Constable bizarrely apologised to the aggressors.

During the period prior to the turning right onto Oxford Street TV footage exists that shows the PSNI officer in charge of the TSG negotiating with myself and other community representatives. Eventually this officer agreed to open the bridge but by this time it was too late.

This again shows PSNI communication and involvement in the facilitation and organisation of what they later termed an illegal offence.

In the week prior to Saturday 19th January the PSNI had much direct and indirect telephone and face to face contact with representatives of those participating in the weekly walk. On the evening of Thursday 17th January the PSNI had made contact via a local minister and asked about the possibility of the Ulster People's Forum using any influence they may have with those partaking in the weekly walk to ensure it went on Saturday 19th January 2013 via Middlepath street and the PSNI gave assurances that there would be no repeat of the mistakes of Saturday 12th January when the PSNI closed the Queens bridge.

This again shows PSNI engagement prior to the commencement of a walk they knew to be illegal. The PSNI at no stage via any of their intermediaries made it be known that the walk was illegal and furthermore they encouraged spokespersons of the Ulster People's Forum to publicly voice their approval for this change of route. They later attempted to prosecute me for encouraging an unnotified public procession. I strongly contend that the PSNI are guilty under criminal law of entrapment by their encouragement of me to ask people to walk a particular route which they knew to be illegal and for which they would later charge me.

The PSNI have been asked for the minutes of these meetings they held with local East Belfast clergy and community representatives which proves their guilt in respect of my allegations. They have refused this request, made by solicitors acting on behalf of Mr William Frazer, under grounds of national security. This is perverse and unacceptable.

   I would ask that the PONI investigate why the PSNI seek to cover up any record of their engagement with community representatives and investigate my allegation that the PSNI facilitated and encouraged an offence which they knew or later found out to be illegal.

   I appreciate that the PONI is not in place to provide Judicial clarity on aspects of the law however I believe it falls within the remit of the PONI to investigate this matter because it hinges not upon whether a person is guilty of an offence or not but whether the PSNI facilitated and encouraged in the prior planning of a walk for which they would later prosecute participants.

   Should the PONI find this to be the case then the matter is not whether the PSNI knew the walk was an offence at the time of their engagement in facilitating it but rather now that the walk has clearly been determined to be illegal, are the PSNI liable to prosecution for a breach of the law?

I would contend that no legislation exists to allow for the bypassing of the law therefore it is now clearly the position that due to the fact the PSNI encouraged and facilitated an illegal act under law they must be liable to prosecution.
The PONI should give due regard to whether the PSNI acted inappropriately and illegally in failing to criminally prosecute those officers that took part in this decision making process.

(B)
The PSNI held a meeting with the Ulster People's Forum along with clergymen Pastor Mark Gordon and Rev Mervyn Gibson on 29th January 2013. The purpose of this meeting was mainly to discuss from our point of view the human rights abuses taking place against the PUL community.
    During the meeting issues were discussed around the blocking of roads with PSNI stating this was illegal.
The UPF gave an undertaking to use any influence they may have had to call for a move to white line protests.
ACC Will Kerr, head of the PSNI criminal justice strategy said that whilst he couldn't be seen to be making any deals in relation to prosecutions he would however review whether it was in the public interest to prosecute those who may have been guilty of obstruction on dates prior to 29th January 2013. ACC Kerr effectively said that should the protests be lawful in terms of white line from 29th January onwards the PSNI would be unlikely to prosecute anyone not already in the system for prosecution prior to this date.

Following the UPF announcement of support for white line protests the **PSNI issued a press statement on 31st January 2013** which was carried in much of the National and local media. In it the PSNI, referring to the meeting held on 29th January said **"Police welcome the fact that legal, peaceful protest was being encouraged and agreed to meet with representatives of the Ulster People's Forum in the future."**
    The PSNI later charged me under section 46 of the serious crime act 2007 for speeches which were made on 5th December 2012 and in the first week of January 2013. Therefore the PSNI had within their possession the evidence of these speeches when they met with a delegation from the UPF, which I was leading on 29th January 2013.

Further to this the PSNI released the statement praising our commitment to and encouragement of **_"lawful and peaceful protest"_** on 31st January 2013. Surely at this time I was under investigation for the contrived charges the PSNI would bring on 29th February 2013 (which would be later dropped amid serious questions around their validity) and therefore it would have been wholly irresponsible of the PSNI to release a public media statement praising the group I represented for encouraging **_"lawful and peaceful protests"_** when in fact they believed and claimed to have evidence, which was sufficient to justify an arrest and charging decision; that I was engaged in illegal activity and inciting others to do the same.

Given that the PSNI devoted many bail objections to bombarding the Judiciary with tales (none of which were even remotely within the realms of reality) of the destabilising influence I had upon society, it seems rather bizarre that the PSNI would praise me as a representative of the Ulster People's Forum for encouraging **_"lawful and peaceful protest."_** At this stage they had evidence within their possession for which they would later bring forth serious criminal charges, was it therefore acceptable to not only meet with me and enter into discussion about the direction of Union Flag protests but further to this to also release a public press statement praising the UPF delegation when PSNI were investigating the leader of that delegation for serious criminal offences related to the incidents which were under discussion at the 29th January 2013 meeting in Musgrave Street Police station?

(C) I strongly contend that the PSNI used this meeting on 29th January to try and gauge what level of influence I was willing to bring to bear and how useful this would be for their strategic aims. I also contend that when the PSNI realised that I would not dance to their tune or agree to use my influence to encourage protests to go in a direction which I did not agree with, they decided to bring forward the charges as a means of silencing political dissent and removing a political problem who was proving unworkable for them.

I have no doubt that the PSNI waited over 2 months to bring charges based on evidence they had held from 5th December 2012 for purely political and strategic policing purposes.

I would request that the PONI seize any internal communication between Gold/Silver/Bronze command of the PSNI and the DULCET public order team, especially with the head of that unit Mr Sean Wright.

I believe that a decision was taken within high levels of the PSNI command structure to arrest me based not upon substantive evidence (as has been proven by the PPS withdrawal of the charges) but upon the need to remove and silence someone who was destabilising the political process and who the PSNI needed removed from the equation to allow other Civic leaders more sympathetic to their position to change the tempo and direction of the Union flag protests.

I request that the PONI investigate what discussions took place between representatives of the NIO and the PSNI in relation to the need to arrest me as well as the aforementioned internal communication between senior command and the DULCET team.

Whilst I understand that PSNI have a degree of operational freedom, the question here is whether the PSNI concocted charges for political purposes and even if the PONI finds they didn't and that they did have grounds for charging, the question remains; was the charges they brought timed strategically for political benefit rather than following the due process?

(D) On the evening of 26th February 2013 the Chief Constable met with a delegation from Sinn Fein.

I believe that my name was raised at this meeting and subsequently Sinn Fein informed the Chief Constable they believed I should be arrested.

I believe that immediately following this meeting the arrest warrant for me was issued and a case file that had been sitting waiting for a decision on the best political time to bring forth the charges was then put into play following the frank discussion with the Sinn Fein delegation.

I contend that it is wholly inappropriate for the PSNI to discuss potential individual cases with outside persons or political parties and therefore there was serious misconduct from the PSNI in how they planned my arrest and I believe the timing of this was influenced by Sinn Fein.

(E) I am aware that during the course of a meeting between Sinn Fein and the Chief Constable on 26th February 2013 my name was brought up and the PSNI discussed with Sinn Fein the best way to deal with me and the political ramifications if I were to be arrested. This is a serious breach of data protection guidelines and given that a number of those within the Sinn Fein delegation were convicted terrorists, I believe the Chief Constable compromised my personal safety by discussing me and a potential case against me with Sinn Fein.

2. Complaints arising from arrest operation & subsequent charging and bail hearing.

OVERVIEW

(A) I allege that the officer representing the PSNI in Belfast Magistrates Court on Saturday 2nd March 2013 committed, with the full knowledge of his superiors, an act of perjury.
   This act played a significant role in the refusal of bail and subsequent removal of my liberty.
   Subsequent to the initial act of perjury I allege that on 8th March 2013 an officer knowingly briefed a Barrister acting on behalf of the PPS wrongly which subsequently led to the same act of perjury that was committed on 2nd March being reinforced by the PPS on 8th March. I believe that the PSNI DULCET team deliberately and purposefully encouraged both these acts of perjury. *(Statements from arresting Police officers support this)*

(B) I allege that the PSNI acted outside of the powers granted to them on the search warrant signed by District Magistrate Mark Hammil that allowed PSNI to enter and search my home address.
   The PSNI seized and searched a car belonging to a third party, namely my Father, from a car park in Kilcooley, Bangor.
They had no warrant to seize any property belonging to my Father nor did they have genuine reason to believe that this car had been used in any offence.

Background the allegations arising in this section:

The allegations of police wrongdoing in this section are directly linked to my arrest and the subsequent bail hearing. A large number of issues from within section 1 of this document deal with the lead up to my arrest and the political motivation behind it. This section raises two serious issues around perjury and an abuse of power by the PSNI.

(A) I was arrested following a lengthy search operation at the home of Pastor Mark Gordon on 28th February 2013.
Pastor Gordon was bizarrely charged with Obstruction by the police but was found not guilty in Newtownards Magistrates Court.

Pastor Gordon has kindly disclosed relevant police statements that are attached to this section. The PSNI took to the witness stand on 2nd March 2013 and whilst under oath the detective Constable told the presiding Judge that I was found in a locked attic.
This was a major part of the Judges summoning up when refusing me bail. This was a blatant lie.

The statements by the arresting officers which are attached to this document show that this was an outright lie.

This was a criminal act of perjury and I believe the Ombudsman has the power within their remit to request criminal prosecution.

I would also like the Ombudsman to investigate my assertion that this act of perjury was carried out with the full knowledge of the officers superiors as given the fact that all the statements from the arresting officers conflict the account the Detective gave to the Court I can only conclude that this act of perjury was a deliberate act contrived by Senior management within the PSNI.

Should the PONI find that this was not a deliberately contrived act then I am still of the view that a clear criminal offence has been committed and ignorance or a mistake is not reasonable defence when dealing with a situation of the magnitude of the refusal of bail and taking of someone's liberty.

(B) The PSNI warrant to search my home on 27th February 2013, granted by District Judge Mark Hammil, allowed for a search of my home, xx xxxxxxx xxxxxx (*address redacted*)
The arresting team, seemingly out of frustration further searched premises in the Kilcooley estate in Bangor.

The PSNI then took the unlawful step of seizing a car that was parked stationary in the car park of Kilcooley Square and took it away for searching.

This car belonged to my Father, xxxxx xxxxx (*Name redacted*). No attempt was made to contact my father in relation to the seizing of his car. I am merely a 3rd party named driver on the insurance policy.

APPENDIX

- **FOI- PSNI bugging of premises and tapping telephones**
- **FOI- Communication with Downing Street**
- **Implications of Haass proposal document**
- **Legal letter from solicitors acting for DPP Barra McGrory**
- **Response to B McGrory Solicitors**
- **Extracts from B McGrory evidence at NI Select Affairs Committee**

Personal, Professional, Protective Policing

FREEDOM OF INFORMATION REQUEST

Request Number: F-2014-03982

Keyword: Operational Policing

Subject: Warrant For Illegal Recording Of Private Conversations

Request and Answer:

Question 1

Does a warrant exist for the illegal recording of private conversations at xxxxx, xxxxxx, Bangor? The
Voluntary Education Forum has been made aware that the PSNI are targeting a specific individual,
namely xxxxx, for covert surveillance with the permission of the cafe owner.

Question 2

Does a warrant exist for the bugging of xxxxxxx telephone?

Answer

In accordance with the Act, this letter represents a Refusal Notice for this particular request. The Police Service of Northern Ireland can neither confirm nor deny that it holds the information you have requested.

Section 1 of the Freedom of Information Act 2000 (FOIA) places two duties on public authorities.
Unless exemptions apply, the first duty at Section 1(1)(a) is to confirm or deny whether the information specified in the request is held.

The second duty at Section 1(1)(b) is to disclose information that has been confirmed as being held.

Where exemptions are relied upon Section 17(1) of FOIA requires that we provide the applicant with a notice which

a) states that fact,
b) specifies the exemption(s) in question and
c) states (if that would not otherwise be apparent) why the exemption applies.

The Police Service of Northern Ireland (PSNI) can Neither Confirm Nor Deny that it holds the information relevant to your request as the duty in Section 1(1)(a) of the Freedom of Information Act 2000 does not apply by virtue of the following exemptions:

Section 23 (5) – Information Supplied By, Or Concerning, Certain Security Bodies
Section 24 (2) – National Security
Section 30 (3) – Investigations
Section 31 (3) – Law Enforcement
Section 40 (5)(b)(i) – Personal Information

Section 40 is an absolute class-based exemption and it is not necessary to carry out a public interest
test in this case.
The release of information under Freedom of Information is a release into the public domain, and not just to the individual requesting the information. Once information is disclosed by FOI there is no control or limits as to who or how the information is shared with other individuals, therefore a release under FOI is considered a disclosure to the world in general.

To confirm that the PSNI hold the requested information would in fact amount to a release into the public domain, of personal information about an individual.

The individual would have no expectation that these details would be released into the public domain, therefore their data protection rights would be breached by release.

Section 23 is an absolute and class-based exemption which means the legislators have determined that there is no requirement to show the Harm in release or to conduct a Public Interest Test.

Sections 24 and 31 are qualified and prejudice-based exemptions meaning that there is a requirement to conduct a Public Interest test and evidence the Harm in release.

Section 30 is a qualified and class-based exemption and it is only necessary to conduct a Public Interest Test.

Harm for Sections 24 And 31
The essence of the work undertaken by the PSNI is to protect both individuals and society as a whole. To confirm or deny whether or not the requested information is even held relates directly to law enforcement and national security.

Any surveillance that may be undertaken by the PSNI is conducted in line with regulatory framework set out in The Regulation of Investigatory Powers Act
2000 (RIPA). Police surveillance activity is subject to annual inspection by the Interception of Communications Commissioners Office (IOCCO) and Office of Surveillance Commissioners (OSC). These inspections assess the PSNI's compliance with the legislation and a full report is submitted to the Prime Minister containing statistical information. To confirm or deny that a warrant does or does not exist would adversely affect law enforcement and would also have an adverse impact on the ability of the PSNI to protect the community, who are at risk from the current terrorist threat.

Factors favouring confirmation or denial S24

The release of the requested information could provide a better understanding of how public funds are spent in relation to national security and could enable the public to make more informed judgements concerning how effectively PSNI use public funding.

Factors against confirmation or denial S24

Confirming or denying that the information is or is not held could impact on national security at a time when the threat level from terrorism is set as SEVERE as well as increasing the risk of harm to the public as already outlined in the Harm above.
Disclosure of the requested information, whether or not it is actually held, would reveal important information on methodology in the use of CHIS whichmay aid those involved in terrorism to adopt methods that may reduce the amount and quality of information/intelligence the PSNI receives.

Divulging whether or not a particular methodology is used by the PSNI and others in protecting National Security would therefore reduce the ability of the
PSNI to effectively protect the safety and well being of the people it serves.

Factors favouring confirmation or denial - S31

Confirming or denying could promote public trust in providing transparency, and demonstrate openness and accountability. This could also satisfy the public that public funds were being used effectively and appropriately particularly in relation to the detection of crime.

Factors against confirmation or denial - S31

The Police Service has a duty to deliver effective law enforcement ensuring the prevention and detection of crime and that the apprehension or prosecution of offenders of justice is carried out appropriately. Confirming whether or not the requested information exists would compromise effective law enforcement issues by revealing methodology with particular reference to the use of such covert tactics. Those intent on terrorist and criminal activity would be able to use the information to avoid detection.

Factors favouring confirmation or denial – S30

There is a public interest in police investigations and how they are conducted. Confirming or denying would better inform the public how the police service may be engaging with its investigative role.

Factors against confirmation or denial – S30

Confirming or denying that a warrant does or does not exist and whether or not someone is the subject of covert surveillance would adversely impact on investigations and alert those involved in crime or terrorism that they have or are have not come to the attention of police. This would provide important information to these individuals who could make plans to avoid detection or continue in the knowledge that police are unaware of their activities.
However, this should not be taken as conclusive evidence that the information you requested exists or does not exist.

Decision

The PSNI has a duty to fulfil its law enforcement function and whilst there is a public interest in the transparency of policing activities the delivery of effective law enforcement is of paramount importance. Confirming whether or not an investigation is taking place or that a warrant does or does not exist could assist those involved in criminal activities to avoid detection, continue in their criminal
activities and frustrate the administration of justice. This is true whether or not information is held relevant to your request.

Although there is strong public interest in knowing how the PSNI fulfils its National Security role and deals with the threat from terrorists there is a greater public interest in ensuring that criminal activities and terrorism are both detected and prevented so ensuring the safety and well-being of the public.

The Service has a duty to protect the community it serves and needs to use exemptions appropriately to protect information if the release of that information would have an adverse impact on the community. The PSNI will not divulge any information which could hinder the prevention and detection of crime and also adversely impact on the apprehension and prosecution of offenders.

I am therefore satisfied that in respect of this request the public interest lies in neither confirming nor denying that any information relevant to your request does or does not exist and that the exemptions at Section 23, 24, 30 and 31 are applicable to this information. This therefore should be considered a refusal notice in relation to this request.

Personal, Professional, Protective Policing

FREEDOM OF INFORMATION REQUEST

Request Number: F-2014-01880

Keyword: Organisational Information/Governance

Subject: Telephone Recordings Chief Constable's Office and Downing Street

Request and Answer:

Question 1
Who was the acting ACC on duty at police HQ on 8th March 2007 between the hours of 7pm and 12 Midnight?

Question 2
Do the PSNI have in their possession any recordings of the telephone conversation between the
Chief Constable's office and Downing Street in relation to two IRA terrorists who had been arrested
on the 8th March?

Answer
PSNI will be cooperating with the review being conducted by Lady Justice Hallett into the administrative scheme for dealing with the 'On the Runs' scheme and has recently given evidence to the Northern Ireland Affairs Committee (Oral evidence: Administrative scheme for 'on-the-runs' HC 1194 Wednesday 7 May 2014). Due to this ongoing investigative effort, PSNI is not in a position to reveal details which may or may not form a part of that work. Therefore in accordance with the Act, this letter represents a Refusal Notice for this particular request. The Police Service of Northern

Ireland can neither confirm nor deny that it holds the information you have requested. We have set out our reasons for this below which explain our decision.

Section 1 of the Freedom of Information Act 2000 (FOIA) places two duties on public authorities.
Unless exemptions apply, the first duty at Section 1(1)(a) is to confirm or deny whether the information specified in the request is held. The second duty at Section 1(1)(b) is to disclose information that has been confirmed as being held.

Where exemptions are relied upon Section 17(1) of FOIA requires that we provide the applicant with
a notice which
a) states that fact,
b) specifies the exemption(s) in question and
c) states (if that would not otherwise be apparent) why the exemption applies.

The Police Service of Northern Ireland (PSNI) can Neither Confirm Nor Deny that it holds the information relevant to your request as the duty in Section 1(1)(a) of the Freedom of Information Act 2000 does not apply by virtue of the following exemption:

Section 30 (3) – Investigations & Proceedings Conducted by Public Authorities

Where Section 30(3) applies it is subject to the Public Interest Test. In a democratic society it is important that any offences can be effectively investigated and prosecuted, as well as allowing the public to have confidence in the ability of the Police Service to uphold the law.

Public Interest Test

Factors Favouring Confirmation or Denial – Section 30
To confirm whether or not there is any information relevant to your request may satisfy the public need to know, at this time, in relation to police

investigations and how they are conducted. Disclosure would better inform the public.

Factors Against Confirmation or Denial – Section 30

By confirming or not that information is held, would in this case disclose what facts may or may not exist in relation to ongoing investigative work. Any police investigation is conducted with due regard to the confidentiality and privacy of any persons involved. Investigation material is exempt for 30 years in case further evidence is uncovered in the future. Confirmation or denial could impede any investigation or impact on the outcome.

Decision

Confirmation or denial of whether the PSNI hold information would amount to a release of information either on this occasion or on other occasions where a similar request is made. Whilst there is a public interest in the transparency of information held by police there is also a strong public interest in maintaining confidence in the PSNI with regard to its handling of information. Any future evidence uncovered could be compromised by disclosure.

It is the view of PSNI that there is a strong public interest favouring neither confirming nor denying that the requested information is held.

No inference can be taken from these statements that the information you requested does or does not exist.

Implications of the Haass proposals

After the Haass talks I took part in a road-show that travelled to various areas and explained the implications of the Haass proposals.
This document was drawn up by the Ulster Human Rights Watch as part of a campaign against those proposals.

Introduction

This document provides a summary analysis of the <u>Haass proposals</u> it also describes the <u>Alternative proposals</u> which would benefit the people of Northern Ireland as a whole, promote their fundamental freedoms and deliver justice for the victims of terrorism. The <u>Haass Proposals</u> constitute only the emerged 'tip of the iceberg' since their implementation would require substantial new legislation in order to create a complex and costly organisation. Understanding the implications of what is proposed by Haass should lead every law-abiding citizen in Northern Ireland to seriously consider and support the <u>Alternatives</u> proposed in this document for freedom of peaceful assembly, the flags and emblems of the State and justice for the victims of terrorism in Northern Ireland.

Understanding the implications of the Haass proposals on

"Flags and Emblems"
<u>(Proposed - A new Commission set-up to deal with a wide range of issues)</u>

1. The proposals on Flags and Emblems are based on the wrong premise, since according to Dr Haass these symbols of sovereignty should be seen in Northern Ireland in the context of the Belfast Agreement signed in 1998.

2. The proposals made by Dr Haass should not be approved for the following reasons:

- The 1998 Belfast Agreement is not a legislative document and as such does not determine the international legal status of Northern Ireland as being part of the United Kingdom.
- The Belfast Agreement was implemented by way of the Northern Ireland Act 1998, which states that Northern Ireland in its entirety remains part of the United Kingdom and shall not cease to be so without the consent of a majority of the people of Northern Ireland voting in a poll.
- Until a majority of the people of Northern Ireland, voting in a poll, decides to join the Republic of Ireland, the only flags and emblems that can legally be flown in Northern Ireland are those of the United Kingdom and of the British Monarchy.
- The new process promoting Irishness, which would progressively eradicate all reference to Britishness, will create more instability within Northern Ireland society and in the medium/long term generate even more public disorder.

3. Whilst nothing could be agreed on Flags and Emblems, it was proposed that a new Commission should be established to discuss the role of identity, culture and traditions in the life of the citizens of Northern Ireland. These issues, which are common to many parts of the United Kingdom, including Northern Ireland society, should not bring into question the constitutional position of Northern Ireland as part of the United Kingdom.

4. The Commission would be dealing with a whole range of issues that have the potential to undermine the internationally recognised status of Northern Ireland as part of the United Kingdom.

5. In addition to flags and emblems, the Commission will be dealing with the Irish language, a Bill of Rights for Northern Ireland, gender issue, public holidays, memorabilia, symbols, emblems and signage displayed in local and central government buildings, symbols of national and other identities, and will also be open to consider other topics.

Conclusion: Since the agreed and legal status of Northern Ireland as part of the United Kingdom has not constituted the basis of all discussions, the setting up of yet again another Commission will only open the floodgate for the consideration of numerous issues that have the potential to adversely affect the rights and fundamental freedoms of the people of Northern Ireland.

Allegiance to the State surrendered

Understanding the implications of the Haass proposals on "Contending with the Past"

(Proposed - The Report of the Consultative Group on the Past (2009) reinstated)]

1. The basis for this proposal concerning the past has been drafted in order to avoid any reference to acknowledging the truth of what happened in Northern Ireland in relation to the terrorist campaign started in 1968, which officially ended in 1998. Instead of stating the existence of terrorism, the proposals substitute words such as "war, conflict or Troubles". The real victims of terrorism, who are entitled to truth, justice and acknowledgement, are not mentioned even once in the Haass proposals.

2. Terrorism was never justified in Northern Ireland and those who wished to see a change in the international status of Northern Ireland should have pursued their political aims by way of the peaceful democratic means that were available to them.

3. In these proposals there is no attempt to define the various categories of victims, particularly the victims of terrorism, so as to best address their needs (page 22 of Haass proposals) and the attempt is made to equate law enforcement officers with terrorists, and make them all equally responsible for what happened during the thirty years terrorist campaign
(page 23 of Haass proposals).

4. It is proposed that a new body, the Historical Investigative Unit (HIU), be established through legislation. All the powers that are at present those of the Historical Enquiries Team, the Police Ombudsman for Northern Ireland and the Police Service of Northern Ireland will be transferred to the HIU for the investigation of historical cases. The HIU will have access to all files and also to intelligence detained by the PSNI (page 27 of Haass proposals). It will be for the HIU to decide whether to refer a case to the Public Prosecution Service. The Policing Board will consider candidates from within and outside Northern Ireland to be appointed as director of the HIU. It is not known who will be employed to carry out the investigative work, although they will apparently not be police officers. There is no reason or guarantee that the HIU will deliver a better outcome than the HET, PONI and the PSNI are currently delivering.

5. The other proposed body is the Independent Commission for Information Retrieval (ICRC) that will be independent from the justice system. The ICRC will be used to provide information to the families of those who were killed.
However, information and documentation retrieved through the ICRC will not be able to be used in prosecutions.
This will, in effect, grant immunity to anybody against whom there is evidence that he/she took part in terrorist activities. Any person who has been involved in acts of terrorism and wishes to escape prosecution will be able to volunteer information (page 31 of Haass proposals), which may not be to the advantage of the victims and their families. The ICRC will be empowered to offer immunity in both civil and criminal courts (page 34 of Haass proposals) and whatever raw information is provided to the ICRC, it will not be disclosed to the judiciary (page 34 of Haass proposals).

6. In addition the ICRC will also have an internal unit to analyse patterns or themes which may well lead to both the rewriting of the history of the terrorist campaign and its justification (page 32-33 of Haass proposals). The ICRC will be staffed with lawyers, historians and academics (page 35 of Haass proposals).

Conclusion: This proposed two-tier system will be to the advantage of those who to this day have escaped the rigour of the law. The Historical Investigative Unit will be a complex and expensive organisation which will control the use of information and intelligence and it is unlikely that it will deliver any satisfactory outcome for the innocent victims of terrorism. The Independent Commission for Information Retrieval will provide for those who have been involved in terrorist activities the ideal means of obtaining complete and final immunity.

Understanding the implications of the Haass proposals on

"Parades, Select Commemorations and Related Protests",

(Proposed - The Hillsborough Agreement (2010) aggravated)

1. The proposals by Haass concerning public assemblies in Northern Ireland are extensively based on those made (and already rejected), resulting from the Hillsborough Agreement (2010), and which have now been extended to apply not only to public processions but also to static meetings designated as *"Select Commemorations"*.

2. What used to be the Office of Public Assemblies, Parades and Protests (OPAPP) and the Public Assemblies, Parades and Protests Body (PAPPB) under the Hillsborough Agreement are now rebranded the Office for Parades, Select Commemorations and Related Protests ('the Office') and the Authority for Public Events Adjudication ('the Authority'). The procedures and rules that apply to the system are essentially the same as those produced in the Hillsborough Agreement, albeit with further constraints imposed on the organiser.

3. In 2010 the Loyal Orders dismissed the proposals made in the Hillsborough Agreement and it must be acknowledged that unfortunately there is nothing more inviting in the Haass proposals to justify the Orders consenting to them. Furthermore, there is nothing in these proposals that would provide a way of effectively addressing and resolving outstanding issues. The failures of the Haass proposals are outlined as follows:

- Nowhere in this proposal is the right to freedom of religion mentioned, as references are made only to the right to freedom of expression. However the High Court of Justice in Northern Ireland stated in the case of Dunloy v Parades Commission that a public procession whose purpose is to attend a religious service *"is a manifestation of religion"*. The Loyal Orders are religious organisations and their right to freedom of religion exercised in conjunction with their right to freedom of peaceful assembly is of paramount importance.
- The proposals do not promote the right to freedom of peaceful assembly but support opposition to the exercise of that right with a variety of arguments. Reference is made to the 'right for everyone to be free from sectarian harassment', which has never been clearly defined and can be used by objectors and protesters as a means to abusively prevent peaceful public assemblies from taking place. Mention is also made of a wide variety of human rights of individuals engaged in or affected by a parade or protest but no attempt is made to determine a balanced approach between the right to freedom of peaceful assembly and the rights of others.
- Although there is an emphasis on the way assemblies should be conducted nowhere in the proposals is there the basic consideration or mention of the right to freedom of peaceful assembly as applying to peaceful assemblies only. Those who organise or take part in any form of public assembly which is not entirely peaceful in intent and practice have no rights under the law and there should be a process for prohibiting these kinds of assemblies from taking place.

- The proposals are constantly focused on the necessity of engagement and face-to-face contact between assembly organisers and objectors/protesters, although in the Dunloy v Parades Commission judgment the Court of Appeal in Northern Ireland stated that *"organisers of processions cannot reasonably be expected to enter into face-to-face dialogue with self-appointed soi-disant "representatives" who are not selected by any proper democratic method* [and] *who may operate on the edge of legality or who may in fact been encouraging vociferous and threatening opposition"*.
- The proposed body making determinations would take into consideration the participation or non-participation of the assembly organiser in face-to-face dialogue or mediation and any explanations offered for non-participation, although today the Parades Commission does not make face-to-face contact between the public procession organiser and people within the locality a requirement.

Conclusion: **The Haass proposals will further seriously undermine the right to freedom of peaceful assembly exercised in conjunction with the right to freedom of religion and the right to freedom of expression for law-abiding people in the context of a democratic society in Northern Ireland.**

Overview of the minimum requirements to be complied with by the Parades Organiser if the Haass proposals are approved and implemented
(based on the Hillsborough Agreement 2010)

Note: You will have 11 Mountains to climb and 53 Hurdles to Jump

Are YOU - the Organiser of this Parade prepared for this Marathon Battle?

Stage (Hurdle) No 1 - Preparation by way of local dialogue:
Local dialogue should start at the earliest possible time without waiting for the notification of the public parade.
The Parades Organiser:

1. Must consider all of the aspects of the parade in advance with a view to identifying and seeking to address all relevant issues which may lead to disputes;
2. Must identify sensitive locations and hold informal discussions with local residents, business people and those with a legitimate interest in the proposed parade prior to submitting formal notification to the Office for Parades, Select Commemorations, and Related Protests;
3. Must seek to address reasonable local concerns about the proposed parade prior to notifying the Office for Parades, Select Commemorations, and Related Protests;
4. Must state the measures he is taking to address relevant issues.

Stage (Hurdle) No 2 - Notification of the public parade:
Notification must be submitted on a form to the Office for Parades, Select Commemorations, and Related Protests by the Parades Organiser at least 25 working days prior to the date of the parade.

The Parades Organiser:
5. Must make every effort to minimise any adverse impact the parade might have on the locality;
6. Should take into consideration places identified in any notified concerns or objections as raising valid human rights issues;
7. Should take into account any place of cultural or religious significance;
8. Should take into consideration places connected to the past conflict;
9. Must consider any sensitive locations that exist in the immediate vicinity of the parade and identify this location on the form;
10. Must state what measures he is taking to address the relevant issues;
11. Must identify those categories of participants and third party participants (eg. Bands) expected to take part in the public parade;
12. Must promptly inform the Office for Parades, Select Commemorations, and Related Protests of the eventual cancellation of the public parade and confirm it in writing;
13. Should submit the notification form as early as possible in order to create as much opportunity as possible for issues to be resolved through face-to-face meetings;
14. Should refer to the late notification and emergency procedures if it is not possible to anticipate the parade in time to give the amount of notification necessary;

15. Must note that it is an offence to knowingly organise a parade for which notice has not been given;
16. Should take note of informal discussions on the notification form that will be considered by the
Authority for Public Events Adjudication if the parade proceeds to adjudication;
17. Should take into account any place where there has been a history of disorder relating to parades or protests.

Stage (Hurdle) No 3 - Notice of concerns or objections:
An objector can submit a notice of concerns and objections form to the Office for Parades, Select Commemorations, and Related Protests within 10 working days after the publication of the notification of the public parade form. Copy of the notice form will be sent to the Parades Organiser by the Office for Parades, Select Commemorations, and Related Protests.
The Parades Organiser:
18. Should read the form carefully with a view to finding a way to address the issues raised, as objectors will have outlined the reasons for their concerns or objections as fully as possible;
19. Should note that failure to comply with the Code of Conduct can be used to justify a notice of concerns or objections for future parades.
Stage (Hurdle) No 4 - Notice of a protest meeting:
The objector who has submitted a notice of concerns and objections can submit on a form a notice of protest meeting to the Office for Parades, Select Commemorations, and Related Protests at the latest 18 working days before the day of the protest.
Stage (Hurdle) No 5 - Local dialogue:
Maximum emphasis is placed on local contact and agreement in the early stages. The principle is that disputes ideally should be resolved by the parties involved as quickly and efficiently as possible.
Face-to-face engagement will be the norm and encouraged as such.
The Parades Organiser:
20. If required, must agree with the objector that a third party chairs the informal discussion between the Parades Organiser and objectors;
21. Must fully justify the exceptional circumstances that prevent him from entering into engagement to the satisfaction of the Authority for Public Events Adjudication if he does not engage;
22. Should note that the Authority for Public Events Adjudication may take into account a refusal to enter into engagement;

23. Must verify the local agreement once it is reached and before he notifies it to the Office for Parades, Select Commemorations, and Related Protests;

24. May choose with the agreement of the objector that a monitor be appointed by the Authority for
Public Events Adjudication and must inform the Office for Parades, Select Commemorations, and Related Protests about this.

Stage (Hurdle) No 6 - Mediation:
If during the period of 10 working days after submission of the notification of concerns and objections form the issues have not been resolved, the process moves to mediation. Face-to-face engagement will be the norm and encouraged as such at this stage.

The Parades Organiser:
25. Should agree with the objector to choose a mediator from the list held by the Office for Parades, Select
Commemorations, and Related Protests;

26. Must fully justify any exceptional circumstances that prevent him from entering into face-to-face engagement to the satisfaction of the adjudication body if he refuses to engage;

27. Should note that refusal to take part in mediation may be considered by the Authority for Public Events
Adjudication;

28. Should note that a monitor will automatically be appointed by the Authority for Public Events
Adjudication to attend the parade if there is agreement on a resolution.

Stage (Hurdle) No 7 - Adjudication:
If no agreement is reached 15 working days before the parade is due to take place the mediator will refer the dispute to the Authority for Public Events Adjudication along with a factual report on the mediation to date. Copies of the reports will be sent to the organiser and objector.

The Parades Organiser:
29. Should continue mediation while the dispute is considered by the Authority for Public Events Adjudication. If mediation produces a decision then the Authority stops considering the issue;

30. has the right to know the case of the objector and is given an opportunity to respond;

31. Should comply with the requirements imposed by the Authority for Public Events Adjudication;

32. Should note that a monitor will automatically be appointed by the Authority for Public Events
Adjudication where there has been a concern or objection lodged.

Stage (Hurdle) No 8 - Review of a panel decision:
The **Parades Organiser** can appeal a decision taken by the Authority for Public Events Adjudication on the grounds of sufficiently relevant or significant evidence.

Stage (Hurdle) No 9 - Judicial review:
A decision by the Authority for Public Events Adjudication may be questioned by way of judicial review, but it should be kept in mind that it is unlikely that the Courts will be willing to consider the merits of any decision by the Authority: judicial review is generally confined to procedural matters or points of law and even if a judicial review application is successful before the Courts, it is unlikely that a court would substitute its own decision for that of the Authority. Rather, it will send the matter back to the Authority to reconsider its decision in line with the directions of the Court on the points of procedure or law on which the Court has ruled.

Note also that most applications for judicial review against the current Parades Commission have been unsuccessful because the Courts have ruled that disputes over parades are matters for determination by the 'expert body' appointed by Parliament for the purpose and that the Courts should not intervene save for said errors of procedure or on points of law.

This provision for judicial review does not therefore provide a proper appeal against decisions of the Authority for Public Events Adjudication.

Stage (Hurdle) No 10 - The Parade takes place (subject to any restrictions agreed through mediation or imposed by the adjudication body):

The Parades Organiser:
33. Must encourage participants to show respect and tolerance and behave with due regard for the rights and traditions of others (music, words, behaviour, clothing and uniforms, flags);

34. Must note that anyone who breaches the requirements set by the Authority for Public Events
Adjudication is guilty of an offence and liable to prosecution;

35. Should take measures to prevent any harassment including that on the grounds of religious belief or political opinion of any person in the vicinity of a parade, whether or not the person is participating in the parade;

36. Should ensure that he keeps a list of all those participating in the parade, including names and contact details for the persons responsible for each organisation;
37. Should make this list available to the PSNI on request;
38. Must ensure that the parade takes place in accordance with the details submitted to the Office for
Parades, Select Commemorations, and Related Protests;
39. Should ensure that changes agreed to through dialogue or mediation are complied with.
40. Should note that failure to comply with agreed changes is a breach of the Code of Conduct;
41. Should note that any failure to comply with requirements imposed by the Authority for Public Events
Adjudication may render the organiser liable to prosecution for an offence under the legislation;
42. Should ensure that there are appropriate numbers of stewards for the parade;
43. Must give guidance and instruction to stewards on their role prior to the parade;
44. Should make every effort to ensure that all participants are informed of the terms of the Code of
Conduct;
45. Should make clear to the participants that any failure to comply with the terms of the Code of
Conduct could lead to them being excluded from future parades;
46. Should comply with any direction given by the PSNI where a public safety issue arises;
47. Should encourage participants to comply with directions regarding public safety;
48. Should ensure that no-one under the influence of alcohol or illegal drugs is allowed to participate in the parade;
49. Should take all reasonable steps to facilitate the monitor's access to the parade once he has been appointed;
50. The Parades Organiser should note that it is an offence to:
- Knowingly organise a parade for which notice has not been given;
- Knowingly organise a parade that differs from the terms notified to the Office for Parades,
Select Commemorations, and Related Protests;

- Fail to comply with the requirements imposed by the Authority for Public Events Adjudication;
- Prevent or disrupt a lawful public assembly;
- Harass persons taking part in a public assembly.

51. The **Parades Organiser** should also note that failure to comply with the Code of Conduct can be used
to justify a notice of concerns or objections for future parades and may be taken into account by the Authority for Public Events Adjudication in future adjudications.

Stage (Hurdle) No 11 - Evaluation:
The evaluation will be compulsory if the Authority for Public Events Adjudication has made a decision on the public parade. It must take place within 60 days of the date of the assembly. The meeting will be chaired by a listed mediator.

The Parades Organiser:
52. Should make every effort to attend the meeting convened by the Office for Parades, Select Commemorations, and Related Protests.
The evaluation will be 'voluntary' if the dispute is resolved at either local dialogue or mediation stage.
But note that an objector or the PSNI can request an evaluation and an evaluation meeting must then be held even if the Parades Organiser disagrees. The meeting will be chaired by a listed mediator.

The **Parades Organiser**, any objector or PSNI:
53. Can request an evaluation after the parade. The Office for Parades, Select Commemorations, and
Related Protests must arrange the meeting within 60 days of the parade taking place.

THE ALTERNATIVE for
"Freedom of Peaceful Assembly in Northern Ireland"

A successful regulation process could be achieved provided that the new legislation applying to public assemblies is based on fundamental principles that conform to the European Convention on Human Rights. The seven principles are as follows:

1. The right to assembly only applies to peaceful assemblies, whether processions, static meetings and/or protests.
Under Article 11.1 of the ECHR, *"everyone has the right to freedom of peaceful assembly"*. The Convention clearly excludes any form of violent assembly or any assembly organised in support of any violent message. Any such violent procession, meeting or protest is unlawful and must not be authorised or tolerated by State authorities. The regulation process should first deal with the prohibition of violent assemblies.

2. The regulation mechanism applied by State authorities must not constitute an interference with the exercise of the right to freedom of peaceful assembly. The European Convention proclaims that: *"everyone has the right to freedom of peaceful assembly"*. This right is acknowledged and guaranteed to everyone who is peaceful in intent and practice and there is no requirement in a democratic society to seek permission from a public authority to exercise it or to have to make a case as to why it should be permitted. However, the European Court has recognised that the State may enforce a notification mechanism in the public interest to prohibit violent assemblies and impose restrictions on peaceful assemblies if necessary.

3. The duty of the State is to protect the right to freedom of peaceful assembly. The duty of the State authorities is to protect the right to freedom of peaceful assembly of those who wish to exercise this right peacefully. The European Court also stated that in a democracy the right to counter-demonstrate cannot extend to inhibiting the exercise of the right to demonstrate. In the case of a violent counter-protest, it is the duty of the State authorities to ensure that the right to freedom of peaceful assembly of those who process or assemble is still effectively exercised.

4. Voluntary engagement.
The Court of Appeal in Northern Ireland has indicated that engagement cannot be understood as an obligation for the public procession organiser to engage in face-to-face dialogue with so-called representatives of the local section of the community. Engagement is and must remain simply an option that the public procession organiser is able to avail of.

5. Restrictions may be imposed on the exercise of the right to freedom of peaceful assembly provided they are prescribed by law, have a legitimate aim and are necessary in a democratic society (ECHR Article 11.2).
Restrictions can only be imposed on the right to freedom of peaceful assembly if it is peaceful; a violent assembly in intent or practice should simply be prohibited. Any restriction imposed by a public authority must conform to the prescription of Art. 11.2. of the European Convention. If the public assembly organiser is to take measures which amount to self-imposed restrictions, these should conform to the same provisions of Art. 11.2.

6. Prohibition of any actions aimed at the destruction of the right to freedom of peaceful assembly (ECHR Article 17).

This important provision of the European Convention prevents public authorities, organisations or individuals from engaging in activities using rights and freedoms, such as the right to private and family life, with the view of destroying or limiting the rights of others in an unnecessary or disproportionate manner. As soon as an organisation or individual engages in such an activity with the aim of destroying the right to freedom of peaceful assembly, they lose the benefit of the rights and freedoms enshrined in the Convention.

7. The review by a higher independent body.
The regulation mechanism should include a regulation body that makes the initial decision and another, independent body empowered to deal with review requests. Once this remedy has been availed of, an application for judicial review could then be made.

THE ALTERNATIVE for
Victims of Terrorism in Northern Ireland

A proper alternative for the victims of terrorism in particular must be based on principles and procedures that ensure that justice is done for all the people of Northern Ireland. The three steps recommended for implementation are as follows:

1. The first step is to acknowledge that whatever grievance some sections of the community may have had in the past, nobody should ever have had recourse to terrorism.

The 30 plus year (and continuing) campaign of terrorism in Northern Ireland, across the rest of the United
Kingdom and in the Republic of Ireland has caused many civilians, security forces personnel, members of the judiciary and of parliament to be murdered or seriously injured, and these victims deserve to see justice done.

2. The second step is to acknowledge that there are different categories of victims resulting from the campaign of terrorism and from the measures taken by law enforcement officers to prevent and repress those engaging in terrorist activities.

The overwhelming majority of victims are the real victims of terrorism. Other victims including those resulting from the illegal or excessive use of force by law enforcement officers should also be recognised. The identification of the various categories of victims will enable the specific social and emotional needs of each category of victims to be efficiently addressed.

3. The third step is to ensure that the four investigation mechanisms already in place continue to operate efficiently, while constantly developing their ability to better identify, arrest and prosecute those responsible for crimes committed in the past.

A. The Historical Enquiries Team (HET) is part of the PSNI and is directly answerable to the Chief Constable. Its responsibility is to re-examine all deaths, particularly of victims of terrorism, that occurred between 1968 and 1998. The HET is presently reviewing its internal procedures according to the recommendations made by Her Majesty's Inspectorate of Constabulary (HMIC). As soon as this is completed, it will resume its investigating work.

The HET seeks to involve the relatives of victims who can direct their queries to the team carrying out the review.

Whenever evidential opportunities are found, the HET can refer the case to the PSNI, which may lead to criminal proceedings being undertaken by the Public Prosecution Service.

B. The Police Ombudsman for Northern Ireland (PONI) carries out investigations into historical cases of unresolved murders that occurred during the terrorist campaign if police conduct was not consistent with the approved standards or allegedly in breach of the law. Cases may be referred by the HET or complaints lodged by individuals.

At the end of the investigation, the Police Ombudsman issues a report.

C. The Attorney General for Northern Ireland has been given the power to direct new inquests into deaths which happened in the past. He has a large degree of discretion. The test imposed by law has a low threshold and considering what is submitted to him he may consider new inquests advisable.

D. The Secretary of State for Northern Ireland may establish new processes with the view of ensuring that the truth is revealed as regards historical cases. In addition, cooperation between investigative authorities in Northern Ireland and public authorities investigating historical cases in the Republic of Ireland can be further developed.

Conclusion: These various bodies and authorities, while independent from one another, specialise in the investigation of the various issues related to historical cases. These must be preserved and constantly improved so as to ensure that the truth is established and justice is done for all victims and particularly the victims of terrorism.

Support this alternative

THE ALTERNATIVE for
Flags and Emblems of the State in Northern Ireland

The people of Northern Ireland, forming one community, have reaffirmed in the referendum of 1998 that
Northern Ireland is part of the United Kingdom, in compliance with the principle of self-determination recognised by Articles 1 and 55 of the Charter of the United Nations (1945) and Article 1 of both the International Covenant on Civil and Political Rights (1966) and the International Covenant on Economic, Social and Cultural Rights. Therefore it should be acknowledged that:

**1. The constitutional status of Northern Ireland is provided in Section 1(1) of the Northern Ireland Act 1998 which states: "It is hereby declared that Northern Ireland in its entirety remains part of the United Kingdom and shall not cease to be so without the consent of a majority of the people of Northern Ireland voting in a
poll."
2. The national flag and emblems are an expression of the authority of the State and by virtue of this authority the fundamental rights of the different sections of the community of the people of Northern Ireland are acknowledged, protected and promoted.
3. In a democratic society and in compliance with the European Convention on Human Rights, the display of any flag, bunting or emblems in Northern Ireland, that are an expression of a violent culture must be prohibited.
4. The display of the United Kingdom Flag and Emblems in Northern Ireland should be founded on the following principles:
A. Northern Ireland in its entirety is legally part of the United Kingdom of Great Britain and Northern Ireland;
B. The people living in Northern Ireland constitute one community, within which there are various sections;
C. The national flag and emblems express the legal status, sovereignty and authority of the State of the United
Kingdom, which guarantees the existence and promotion of fundamental rights that apply to all members of the community in Northern Ireland;
D. The Union flag and emblems must be allowed to be displayed in all public buildings and grounds for the expression of the legal status, sovereignty and authority of the State and for the commemoration of national historical events;
e. The display of flags, emblems and bunting which is an expression of violent cultures must be prohibited in all public places in Northern Ireland.**

CONCLUSION
For the good of society there are alternatives to the Haass proposals that can be chosen by the people of

Northern Ireland in order to protect and promote fundamental freedoms to peaceful assembly, religion and expression; to improve existing investigating mechanisms; to secure justice, particularly for the victims of terrorism; and to maintain the flags and emblems of the State in Northern Ireland, which is by law in its entirety part of the United Kingdom. The alternatives proposed in this document are presented for your serious consideration and support.

Support these alternatives for Parades, the Past and Flags and Emblems

Demand to remove tweets about the DPP & Public Prosecution service.

*Mr McGrory later told Kate Hoey MP during the NI Select Affairs committee hearing that he had indeed used public funds to pursue this Civil action (extracts from the minutes of this meeting is included). The PPS have also been forced to admit this following a FOI request which is also contained in the appendix of this book.

....

From: XXXXXXX (email address redacted)
Date: 6 June 2014 18:53:55 BST
To: XXXXXXXXX (email address redacted)

Subject: Twitter Receipt of Correspondence

Dear Mr Bryson,

We have received a complaint from Johnson Solicitors on behalf of the Northern Irish Director of Public Prosecutions, Barra McGrory QC, regarding specific content posted on your Twitter account, @jamiebrysonCPNI.

The complaint alleges the attached Tweets are abusive and defamatory in violation of local law in Northern Ireland, and requests the removal of those Tweets. .

If you do not remove the reported content, we may be forced to take action on your account and the matter may be progressed further via defamation proceedings
Please let us know by replying to this email immediately and let us know whether you will voluntarily comply with the request.

NOTE: The Twitter Rules state that users agree to comply with all local laws regarding their online conduct and acceptable content. Users are not permitted to post content deemed unlawful in their local jurisdiction.

This notice is not legal advice. You may wish to consult legal counsel about this matter.

Sincerely,

XXXXXXXXXXX (name redacted)

Response to legal letter from solicitors acting on behalf of DPP McGrory:

7 June 2014

Dear XXXXXXXX (name redacted)

In the past few days I have received correspondence stating that your firm, acting on behalf of the Director of Public Prosecutions Mr Barra McGrory QC, are demanding the removal of tweets from a twitter account registered to my name.

Firstly I am shocked that the DPP could take legal action so quickly, given that the PPS, in conjunction with the PSNI, have taken 16 months to decide whether to bring a jay walking case against me!

This legal action is a perverse attempt to silence the right of the ordinary person to hold to account and to criticise the actions of a publicly accountable body, who in essence are little more than glorified civil servants.

I believe that the PPS are a one sided & biased prosecution service who has waged a war of criminalisation on the law abiding Protestant people.
I also believe that the leader of this organisation was put into his position following a sordid deal cooked up during the Hillsborough agreement.
The last I heard it was not illegal to 'believe' and publicly voice a legitimate concern!

I will not be apologising for making the public aware of Mr McGrorys activities as a solicitor. He DID act on behalf of many IRA terrorists; in fact he acted on behalf of the majority of the IRA's higher echelons and was chosen by that organisation to represent their OTR terrorists.

Your firm also have the sheer audacity to demand the removal of tweets where I merely say "serious questions need asked of the PPS", when I question the impartiality of the PPS, when I highlight that the PPS have dropped charges against IRA terrorists and when I question their shambolic handling of my case.
Just who do you and Mr McGrory think you are?
This kind of action to silence any dissent would not have been out of place in 1930's Germany!

You have effectively sent me a letter demanding the removal of any tweets relating to the PPS or B McGrory. I am sending this back to you to inform you that you can tell Barra McGrory that I will not be removing any general tweets about

the PPS or their impartiality.
I will consult with the legal team and if any tweets breach the law, which I don't believe they do, then I will take further action.

I must ask why the DPP is going to such lengths to try and stop me publicly highlighting the actions of the PPS. Perhaps the real problem is that I am very close to the truth in much of what I say!

If the PPS want to take a law abiding British citizen to Court to try and stop this citizen from holding a public body to account then you go right ahead.
I have £1.37 in my bank account, I will drop it up to your offices and you can pass it into Mr McGrory. Consider me sued for all I have!

Jamie Bryson

FOI (Barra McGrory legal case)

Our Ref: FOI 151/14

Date: 02/07/14

Dear Mr Bryson

I refer to your email dated 8th June 2014, which was received by the PPS FOI team on 09th May 2014, in which you asked for information on who paid for legal services with regard to legal letters sent to Jamie Bryson in relation to Twitter comments and was Mr McGrory acting in his role as DPP or as an individual.

This request has been dealt with under the terms of the Freedom of Information Act 2000.

Freedom of Information Act 2000

The Freedom of Information Act creates rights of access for any person making a request for information to a public authority. The rights of access are twofold. First, to be informed by the public authority if it holds information of the description specified in the request, and if that is the case, secondly, to be provided with that information. These rights are subject to important limitations, which are designed to achieve a proper balance between the right to know and considerations of law and policy in the broader public interest.

You had asked the following:-

Barra McGrory QC engaged the services of Johnson Solicitors to issue legal letters to Jamie Bryson in relation to Twitter comments. Johnson solicitors demanded, on behalf of B

McGrory, the removal of a number of tweets. A percentage of these tweets referred only to the PPS & not to Mr McGrory as an individual. In light of this I would ask who paid for these legal services and was Mr McGrory acting in his role as DPP or as an individual?

In response I can advise that the legal services will be paid by the Public Prosecution Service and Mr McGrory was acting in his capacity as DPP to protect the administration of justice in this jurisdiction and the office of Director of Public Prosecutions.

If you are dissatisfied in any way with the handling of your request, you have the right to request a review in accordance with our review procedure. In the event that you require a review to be undertaken, you can do so by writing to the Assistant Director (Policy), Public Prosecution Service, Belfast Chambers, 93 Chichester Street, Belfast, BT1 3JR or alternatively by sending an e-mail to info@ppsni.gov.uk. You should state clearly the grounds on which you are requesting the review.

Yours Sincerely,

PPS FOI Section

Extracts from Barra McGrory QC's evidence (NI Select Affairs committee hearing regarding OTR's scheme)

*The following extracts prove that Barra McGrory QC did not declare the fact that he represented all of these receiving comfort letters as part of the IRA OTR scheme. Mr McGrory did not declare this vital information prior to his appointment or at any stage thereafter. I raised this matter for quite some time and finally members of the NI Select Affairs committee raised the matter with Mr McGrory.

Q1345 Oliver Colvile: Mr McGrory, thank you very much for coming to talk to us. What you have said so far is very helpful. Can you talk me through how you got the job? You were appointed by the Attorney-General. Was that the British Attorney-General or the Northern Irish Attorney-General?

Barra McGrory: The Northern Irish Attorney-General.

Ian Paisley: They are both British, by the way.

Q1346 Oliver Colvile: Sorry, perhaps I should have put it this way: the Whitehall Attorney-General. Were you head-hunted for the job, or did you have to apply for it by submitting a CV, as most people do?

Barra McGrory: I applied for the job. It was advertised in the press. Under the current justice architecture for Northern Ireland, the Attorney-General has responsibility for the appointment of the Director of Public Prosecutions, but he went about it in a very open and fair way by setting up a selection panel, which he chaired. On it were the Lord Advocate of Scotland at the time, now Dame Elish Angiolini, the then chief inspector of criminal justice, Michael Maguire, who is now the ombudsman, and the then president of the Law Society, Mr Brian Speers. It was a competition, and others were interviewed.

Q1347 Oliver Colvile: Obviously, you had previous knowledge about the names of the people who had been submitted to potentially receive these letters.

Barra McGrory: It was the furthest thing from my mind when I applied for this post.

Oliver Colvile: I am sure.

Q1348 Lady Hermon: You did not declare on your application form your involvement in the OTR scheme.

Barra McGrory: There was no question on the application form which would have
indicated any need to declare it. In my professional life I have been involved in many,
many different types of case, and there was no need.

Q1349 Lady Hermon: So you were just keeping your fingers crossed that the Mr Downey case would not happen, and therefore the OTR scheme would not see the light of day. Did you just keep your fingers crossed?

Barra McGrory: Not at all, Lady Hermon. I had no knowledge of Mr Downey's existence until Mr Justice Sweeney's judgment.

Q1350 Lady Hermon: But you had knowledge of the OTR scheme and you did not disclose that in an application to become the senior prosecutor, the DPP, in Northern Ireland. You kept that quiet.

Barra McGrory: There was no question on the application form that would have required such a declaration. I have been involved in countless cases and given advice to countless people on very sensitive matters, and there was no basis whatsoever on which I would have been expected to make such a declaration.

Q1351 Oliver Colvile: What ended up happening is that you got the job and you had
knowledge of the people you had put forward, because you had been the gatekeeper for Sinn Fein. That ended up going through, but did you not at any stage know what the outcome was for those people? Didn't you know whether they had been accepted or denied?
Barra McGrory: No.

Q1352 Oliver Colvile: In so doing, have you at any stage, as Director of Public Prosecutions, asked the Northern Ireland Office, or whoever you have to go to, who is on that list? If I were the director of Director of Public Prosecutions—I am not a lawyer, so I am talking from a sense of ignorance—I would want to know who was on the list. If you take a case and have to decide whether to prosecute people, you would want to know who might or might not have received a letter that said, "You're okay, chaps. You have the 'get out of jail free' card." Have you ever asked for that information?

Barra McGrory: My office knows the names of people who got the letters, so there was no need for me to ask. It is all documented, and we have already had one case in which someone claimed he was immune from prosecution as a consequence of this scheme. That failed, so my office prosecuted him.

Q1353 Oliver Colvile: So your office does have a list of all those people?

Barra McGrory: Yes.

Q1405 Chair: Could I come back to the advice that you gave on the scheme? You admitted that you gave advice on the scheme. Did you at any stage suggest that it should merely be an evidential test and not the intelligence test? Did you insist that it was an evidential test rather than the wider intelligence-based test—that the police had no intelligence on your clients?
Was that the sort of advice? You hesitate.

Barra McGrory: I don't think I can answer the question.

Q1406 Lady Hermon: Why?

Barra McGrory: First, it strays into issues of privilege in terms of what discussions may or may not have taken place between me and my clients, and I can also say that I have not sought to refresh my memory of those discussions.

Q1407 Lady Hermon: You have wilfully not sought to refresh your memory so that you can come before a Committee and say you don't recall

Barra McGrory: No, no, no.

Q1408 Lady Hermon: Why would you not seek to refresh your memory when you know that you are giving evidence to Lady Justice Hallett and when you know that you are giving evidence to this Select Committee? What is the advantage of that?

Barra McGrory: Because those discussions are covered by legal professional privilege and I do not think it would be appropriate that I do so.

Q1409 Lady Hermon: The interesting thing of course is that you are unable to refute
categorically that you gave advice on whether in fact it should be an evidential test or an intelligence-based test. That is why it is interesting.

Barra McGrory: I am not even allowed to confirm or deny it.

Q1410 Lady Hermon: After you became DPP you knew that there is a statutory duty—a statutory duty—to uphold public confidence in the impartiality and independence of the criminal justice system in Northern Ireland. I am very concerned about your earlier reply to my question that in your application to become the DPP of Northern Ireland, you didn't disclose it because there wasn't a question on the application form. But with hindsight you now know how very damaging the whole revelation around the Downey case has been to public confidence and the rule of law in Northern Ireland. Surely, you should have been circumspect when you were applying to become the DPP, in which we have to have complete confidence—all sides of the community have to have complete confidence in you as DPP—and that should have been disclosed on your application form.

....

Q1425 Ian Paisley: No, while you would not advise someone to go and shred them, you are implying that they are largely worthless from a prosecutorial point of view. Are you suggesting by that that Sinn Fein engaged in a process where they sold their mates a pup?
"We'll get you a letter. You'll be out of the system. Everything will be all right." Is that essentially what you guys were participating in and playing?

Barra McGrory: I wasn't participating in anything. Are you asking me to comment on that?

Q1426 Ian Paisley: Of course I am. I am asking you a straight question. This was a process for Gerry Adams's mates. Were his mates sold a pup—by Gerry—for political purposes?

Barra McGrory: That's between him and them, I suppose.

Q1427 Ian Paisley: No, it's not. Your hands are on this.

Barra McGrory: I don't know in what terms Mr Adams—

Q1428 Ian Paisley: You are his solicitor. You give him advice. Way back, you were giving him advice. This process emerged. You put the names into the process, and they obviously went to you in good faith. "We've got a lawyer on our side. Everything's hunky-dory here."
Fast forward to today. You have used the words, "little legal significance" and "not entirely worthless". You have said that the confidence of those who have them should be abated; that they should be aware that they may not still apply; and that the letters are not an impediment to prosecution anyway. You said all those things today, so effectively the people who received those letters have been sold a pup.

Abbreviations

UPF- Ulster Peoples Forum

PSNI- Police Service of Northern Ireland

RUC- Royal Ulster Constabulary

SOS- Secretary of State for Northern Ireland

IO- Investigating Officer

DUP- Democratic Unionist Party

TUV- Traditional Unionist Voice

PUP- Progressive Unionist Party

UUP- Ulster Unionist Party

IRA- Irish Republican Army

COBRA- Cabinet Office Briefing Room A

DPP- Director of Public Prosecutions (Northern Ireland)

PPS- Public Prosecution Service (Northern Ireland)

Printed in Great Britain
by Amazon.co.uk, Ltd.,
Marston Gate.